Uphill

Helping Students Who Struggle in School

Both Ways

Crystal M. England

HEINEMANN
Portsmouth, NH

Heinemann
A division of Reed Elsevier Inc.
361 Hanover Street
Portsmouth, NH 03801–3912
www.heinemann.com

Offices and agents throughout the world

Library of Congress Cataloging-in-Publication Data
England, Crystal M.
    Uphill both ways : helping students who struggle in school /
Crystal M. England.
        p.   cm.
    Includes bibliographical references.
    ISBN 0-325-00555-9 (pbk.)
    1. Children with social disabilities—Education—United States.
    2. School failure—Social aspects—United States.   I. Title.
    LC4091 .E54 2004
    371.9'0973—dc22   2003018488

Editor: Lois Bridges
Production: Lynne Reed
Cover design: Night & Day Design
Cover illustration: Trisha Payne Ferris
Typesetter: Kim Arney Mulcahy
Manufacturing: Steve Bernier

Printed in the United States of America on acid-free paper
08   07   06   05   04   VP   1   2   3   4   5

To Mom and Dad . . .

*And to Alexander, for his continued optimism
on the journey up the hill*

CONTENTS

ACKNOWLEDGMENTS

I'd like to acknowledge my editor, Lois Bridges, for her ongoing and enthusiastic support. Her energy, insights, and almost instantaneous responses to email make writing a true joy.

I'd also like to thank all those in my life who recognize that writing is a labor of love—sometimes more of one than the other. Kristin, Randy, and Ken . . . your encouragement and your belief in me are treasures. My gratitude also goes out to Jim, for long hours spent listening, discussing, and loving.

And finally, I'd like to express my appreciation to my students during the 2001–2003 school years. It is a privilege to include your names in my book: Mike Biskupski, Amanda Carey, Jon Cass, Nicole Dorn, Drew Fredrickson, Trevor Hast, Shane Hegner, Nick Mulroy, Tiffany Lautenschlager, Christine Taycher, Jon Vorpahl, and to our resident artist, Alvaro.

INTRODUCTION
Jack and Jill Went Up the Hill

Create a picture in your mind of a grassy green hill set against a bright blue sky. Picture two young children, buckets in hand, giggling as they romp up the hill. They pause occasionally to rest. After all, it is a long way to the shiny red well at the top of the hill. Suddenly, and seemingly without warning, the picture changes. Your eyes meet with the vision of children frantically scrambling to right themselves as they speed down the hill. They scrape their elbows and knees and their gathering buckets lurch out of their wiggling grasps.

We all know what happened to poor Jack and Jill after that fateful trip up to the top of the hill. We've all heard of the long fall down and the broken crown. What we do not ever read about is the cause of the fall or the aftermath. Just what precipitated the disaster? Did Jack have an untied shoe? Was he dreaming? And afterward, did Jack receive medical help? Did he want to try to climb the hill again? Was Jill resilient enough to begin the long trudge with renewed energy? And, perhaps most important, why would anyone build a well atop a hill in the first place?

Picture again the grassy hill. The giggling children. The bright blue sky. Instead of a shiny red well, though, there is a sturdy wooden schoolhouse atop the hill. Some of the children are young and hopeful. Their eagerness to fill their buckets with knowledge is readily apparent. Others seem burdened. It is as if they have walked the path before and are weary of the journey. Still others sit stubbornly, refusing to walk another step. They are disappointed in the schoolhouse before they even get inside. Suddenly, the air is pierced by a child's cry. A hapless child has begun her unfortunate descent to the bottom of the heap. A few of the older children, the ones with experience in their eyes and grass stains on their own clothing, know that she will not be strong enough to try to climb the hill again.

Why do some children fall from the grasp of the schoolhouse? What makes some children get up and start the uphill climb all over again while others simply sit in silence? Can the falls be prevented? Can the risks be minimized? Can some of the obstacles that stand in the way of eager children be removed? This book will answer those important questions.

This book, too, will strive to address the issues inherent in the most vital question of the scenario: why is the schoolhouse located in a spot that is an uphill climb no matter the approach? What are the factors that keep education anchored? Why does it seem that more children are falling down the hill than ever before? And who will speak for those children?

My goal is for this book to be both pragmatic and thought provoking. I want readers to feel moved beyond rhetoric towards real reform. At the same time, I wish to offer a practical guide for helping the students who struggle each day in our classrooms. I have known many Jacks and many Jills and I am sure that you have, too. In a way, this is really the book that Jack wrote. Or rather, it is the book that Jack could have written if the educational system hadn't sent him careening down the path to a broken crown.

CHAPTER ONE

CREATING CONDITIONS FOR LEARNING

Recognizing and Removing Practices
That Harm Students

WHEN IT SAYS LIBBY'S . . .

Breathe. Push. Just a little more now! The anticipation builds until an infant's cry is heard. "It's a girl," the doctor exclaims as the excited new parents receive their daughter into their arms. Even before the umbilical cord is cut, she has been given her first label.

It is difficult, if not impossible, to write a book about children without including some labels. We live in a complex society that uses labels to separate, segregate, quantify, and justify. There are labels affiliated with gender, with culture, with religious belief, and with socioeconomic status. Some labels are factual while others are subjective.

Subjective labeling is a risky business. There is a fine line between an accurate adjective and an offensive characterization. Lawsuits asserting slander are prevalent in our litigious society. The old adage about performing to the level of expectation certainly merits care in labeling. A "gifted" musician certainly holds more promise than an average one. An "at-risk" child certainly poses more threat than a high achiever. Or does she? It is the task of all individuals to think

1

beyond the label. At best, the adjectives that we assign one another tell us something about content. At worst, they tell us something about quality. *But only if we let them.*

I've started this book on students who struggle with a brief opinion on labels because I am challenged by the acronyms and jargon that we place upon our students in our schools. When asked what I teach, I like to give the answer "children" . . . but I am nearly always given an eye roll and the answer, "Well, of course, but *what* do you teach?" This means the listener wants to hear about eighth-grade social studies or fourth-grade language arts. The answer "special education" invariably causes a pause and an exclamation of "You must have so much patience." In recent years, when my students are now labeled "at-risk" by their educational environment, I find myself with little answer beyond "children." The students I teach struggle in school for a wide variety of reasons, most notably because it is the educational system and not the students that is "at-risk." But the labels that the students bear open a forum for communication. They give us a starting point for discussion. And so, they are present throughout the book. Read them with an open mind and an eye on some future time when teachers everywhere will find themselves answering, "I teach children."

WHERE THE STRUGGLE MEETS THE ROAD

There are several factors that cause students to struggle in school. Research typically reflects only a segment of a child's life. For example, the presence of books in a child's home is an indicator of early success in school. Parent commitment and follow-through on issues such as school attendance or homework translate to increased success in middle school. Success in high school is linked directly to student motivation. Typically, struggle is addressed yearly but quantified only after failure has been achieved. Data on the factors affecting school completion show the following characteristics to be relevant among students at-risk for not completing high school:

- Living in high-growth states

- Living in unstable school districts

- Being a member of a low-income family

- Having low academic skills (though not necessarily low intelligence)

- Having parents who are not high school graduates

- Speaking English as a second language

- Being single-parent children

- Having negative self-perceptions; being bored or alienated; having low self-esteem

- Pursuing alternatives: males tend to seek paid work as an alternative; females may leave to have children or get married[1]

These factors are only the umbrella for the host of reasons that students struggle in school. How does Jamie get low academic skills? How does Ling overcome her language barriers? Why does Gerald bury his head in his hands and say that he just can't achieve? Certainly, these children can be affected by the circumstances in the preceding list. In fact, at least 58 percent of students who graduate from high school are affected by at least one of the above factors.[2]

So why is it that some students succeed and others struggle? There has been much research done in recent years on resiliency in youth. In the strictest sense, resiliency research refers to a body of international, cross-cultural, developmental studies that followed children born into seriously high-risk conditions. In these families, parents were mentally ill, alcoholic, abusive, or criminal, or were residing in communities that were poverty-stricken or war-torn. The astounding finding from these long-term studies was that at least 50 percent—and often closer to 70 percent—of youth growing up

3

in these high-risk conditions did develop social competence despite exposure to severe stress and did overcome the odds to lead successful lives. Research further tells us that resiliency is fostered by an emphasis on forming caring relationships, having consistently high expectations, and promoting meaningful engagement in home, school, and community.[3]

It should be encouraging that the educational system seems to be meeting the needs of so many students. After all, school completion is a positive indicator that young adults feel supported and prepared to merge into the adult world, right? Perhaps not. In recent years, the Search Institute of Minneapolis, Minnesota, has focused its efforts upon comprising a list of forty developmental assets that all youth should ideally possess. The assets are broken into external and internal assets and further clustered into categories. The assets include the areas of commitment to learning, positive identity, support, and empowerment. According to surveys done on almost one hundred thousand sixth- to twelfth-grade students during the 1996–1997 school year, the average young person experiences only eighteen of the forty assets. In general, older youth have lower average levels of assets than their younger peers. And boys experience fewer assets than girls. Sixty-two percent of all students experience fewer than twenty of the forty critical developmental assets.[4]

IN NO CONDITION TO LEARN

Is it coincidence that what kids need developmentally aligns with what they need to be resilient? Of course not. This leads to the question that responsible educators must ask themselves: is the current condition of education just that—conditional? In a system of checks and balances, overrun with test scores and underfunded with regard to basic needs, it is very important that students be passive receptors of knowledge who do well on standardized exams. The trend of four-year-old kindergarten means that schools are getting children at earlier ages, giving teachers more time to mold young minds into the open vessels that they need to be. Please note the use of the word *need*. We do not seem to have the luxury of allowing children to become the learners they want to be, the dreamers they wish to be, or the expressive thinkers that they ought to be. Author Judy Loken refers to the "Superkid" phenomenon that has swept through our public schools. A superkid is a hurried child—in every sense of the word: hurried to babysitters, hurried to piano lessons, hurried to gymnastics, hurried to soccer, hurried to dance lessons, hurried to achieve, hurried to grow up. No longer are these childhood years to be frittered away in fun and games. No longer are these impressionable years to be wasted in fantasy and creativity.[5]

In "The Hurried Child, Revisited," author Carleton Kendrick (2000) offers that the call-to-arms issued fifteen years ago by David Elkind (1989) in his groundbreaking book, *The Hurried Child,* has unfortunately gone unheeded. Frighteningly, today's hurried child is much more hurried. Kendrick went on to ask, "How are our children responding to our forcing them to grow up fast, as we insist we are simply trying to make them more 'competent'?" Consider these facts:

- Teens are killing themselves and each other at triple the rate they were twenty years ago.
- Teen pregnancy rates in the United States are the highest for any Western nation.
- Fourth-grade girls are dieting in record numbers.
- Serious sports-related injuries have increased several-hundred-fold.
- Twenty percent of youngsters are "flunking" kindergarten.
- Millions of children are medicated daily to make them more "educable" and "manageable" in school and at home.[6]

I remember a television commercial from when I was a young child. It was set in the early morning hours in a large city. A groaning man left his warm bed before the crack of dawn, muttering to himself as he hastily threw on his clothes, intent upon the mission that had beckoned to him at so early an hour. The words he said were, "Gotta make the donuts." Sometimes, I think educators have embraced that same philosophy. Spurred by the fear of high-stakes tests, driven by an ever increasing array of curricular content standards, and dedicated to the lives of children, we rise from our beds each morning, intent on a new day full of opportunities to "educate the children."

TESTING—ONE, TWO, THREE

Unfortunately, forces at the far ends of our controls have made the process of education a very conditional one. Consider the false accountability offered by the current educational injunctions of standards-based reform, high-stakes testing, and the No One Is Left Behind the Child plan. Americans are lulled into believing that a combination of structure and expectation alone will produce learning in all students. If mandates were enough to motivate, our schools would already be overflowing with summa cum laude graduates. There is certainly no harm in following an educational roadmap. Goals and objectives, in their purest form, provide a frame for the variety of teaching strategies and learner needs that are omnipresent in every classroom. However, a system of checks and balances is inappropriate at best and destructive to disadvantaged learners at worst. Author Henry Levin (1986) addressed the educational inequities experienced by some groups of learners nearly twenty years ago with these words:

> The unique needs of the educationally disadvantaged cannot be fully or effectively addressed by reforms of a general nature, such as increasing course requirements, raising teacher salaries, or increasing the amount of instructional time. While these reforms may be desirable on their own merits, they should not be viewed as a substitute for direct and comprehensive strategies to solve

6

the problems of the disadvantaged. In the absence of specific remedial programs for the disadvantaged, the general reforms may overwhelm the abilities of ever larger numbers of them to meet the requirements for high school completion.[7]

In short, a carrot-and-stick approach to educational standards will only serve to further stratify learners. While the media paints pictures of desperate students fleeing the failing public schools that have held them captive against their will, policymakers are able to hide behind a multitude of unachievable standards while whispering, "I told you so." In large part, the disadvantaged in our public schools are not educationally impaired, they are sociologically burdened. A change of environment, a list of expectations, and the pressure of performance on a high-stakes assessment don't feed a physical hunger, shelter a homeless child, or heal a battered heart. Testing the afraid until they become the ashamed is a prescription for failure. It is also the beginning of a risk spiral that has no conceivable ending point.

In *None of Our Business*[8] (2003) I shared the story of a seventh-grade at-risk student who had tears in her eyes as she asked me, "When I fail this test, like I know I will, will you call the test company and tell them that I'm smart?" A year later, in eighth grade, my students were more practical than philosophical. They shrugged a great deal and expressed gratefulness that testing got them out of homework. They filled in their answers rapidly and laid their heads on their desks. They doodled. They drew. And they didn't care. Whether it was the onset of teenage angst or the compilation of years of testing that they'd long ago deemed useless, the disenfranchisement was palpable. Is the vicious cycle of high-stakes testing not apparent? Risk behaviors beget testing. Testing begets risk behavior. It doesn't take a rocket scientist to see the implicit harm in this arrangement. Apparently, it doesn't take a politician, either.

Finally, the physical and environmental concerns prevalent in many schools inhibit the success of the educational endeavors within the four walls that house the children.

Even passive vessels cannot be fulfilled in unfit conditions. Inequalities in access to resources and opportunities still plague U.S. schools. There are schools across the nation where teachers are untrained, key curriculum offerings are lacking, students must use decades-old textbooks or none at all, where teachers do not have enough paper to make photocopies, where vermin and roaches are commonplace, where libraries are closed, where there are no computers in the classrooms, where art and music classes have been cut from the budget, where the bathrooms are locked during the school day because they don't work or lack supplies, and where paint is peeling off the walls and tiles are falling from the ceilings.[9]

WHERE IS MY PENCIL NOW?

I ordered four gross of No. 2 pencils this year. That's 144 pencils per quarter that the students can use, lose, and find again. Like the millions of socks that brave the washing machine each year, never to be heard from again, there is some cosmic force in my classroom (and in the surrounding hallways) that has an enormous appetite for lead.

I have a cupboard in my classroom dubbed "The Kid Cupboard." In it are most of the school supplies that a student may need on any given day. There are markers and crayons and stacks of fresh paper. There are rulers and erasers, extra textbooks when I have them, and those 576 pencils that I already mentioned. The students do not need permission to get supplies from the cupboard. It is, in every sense of the word, "theirs."

I have never told anyone that I work with that I order so many pencils. I know that I would scarcely get the words out of my mouth before a traditionalist would tell me that I am enabling the students. My abrupt answer of "So what?" would probably do little to assist me in keeping a respected position among my colleagues.

"So what," however, is exactly how I feel. I just counted the pencils in the holder atop my desk. There are thirty-three pencils. Thirty-three is *a lot* of pencils for a writer who uses her computer to compose. But they are there when I need a pencil and that knowledge allows me to think more freely and with greater flow. Students, too, need to have the supplies necessary to accomplish the tasks that we give them. It makes little sense to me to reduce education to acts of responsibility or irresponsibility alone. Yet how many times do we practice "tough teaching" in the name of not enabling our students? If students are unprepared for class we shrug and tell them, "Too bad. You'll need to do this on your own time, then." Or we send them to their lockers with scolding admonitions that detract from any motivation they may have had to accomplish the assignment initially.

It is important to help children learn responsible behavior. It is critical that they receive opportunities to practice that behavior and it is integral that natural and logical consequences play a role in their education. However, the teaching of responsibility should not be a condition of learning. In his *Seven Habits of Highly Effective People*,[10] Stephen Covey (1990) encourages readers to "Begin with the end in mind." So it is with the teaching of character traits. Educators must have a clear idea of the affective traits that they wish to cultivate. In addition, there is a great deal of pressure to bestow a plethora of academic content standards. Too often, students are inundated with having to learn too much too quickly. They are being given instructions on how to construct wings as they are pushed off the branches of the tree. They must face peril or soar. The educational question becomes one of *enough*. Can we give them *enough* knowledge? *Enough* resilience? *Enough* motivation? Moreover, will they come to us with *enough*? Over eleven million children live in poverty and *the number of children living in poverty has increased by three million since* 1979.[11] The fastest-growing group of homeless people consists of families with children. Today, families make up about 36 percent of the people who become homeless.[12] In 2000, three million referrals concerning the welfare of approximately five million children were made to Children's Protective Services (CPS) agencies throughout the United States—and this figure reflects only the *reported* abuse within the U.S.[13]

Students who struggle in school often do not have enough background information, enough skills, enough support, or enough opportunity to learn before they are sent to flight or fright. It is bad enough that students drop out of school perpetuated by their own sense of helplessness. The current inappropriate trend of funding linked to failure has also created conditions in which schools are pushing out learners before graduation. This allows them not to report test scores for those students. In March of 2000, with the panic of high-stakes assessment at their heels (and the enrollment needs for the school year already met), schools in Birmingham, Alabama, pushed 522 students out of their schools. The students were "voluntarily withdrawn," but articulated that there was no real choice.[14] Somehow, I don't think that this is the end that any of us have in mind.

THE EDUCATIONAL EQUATOR

You won't find it on any map, but I am certain that there is an educational equator. That is, there is an invisible line that separates students in the primary grades from those in the intermediate grades and beyond. Apparently, it is a magic line that once crossed, gives students a sense of responsibility and attentiveness that they were not expected to evidence only three months before they entered fourth grade. It's as if we say to them, "Abracadabra! You're almost grown now and the rules are different." Instead of shaping behavior by praising our eighth graders when they do come to class with a pencil, we punish them for forgetting. These students have crossed the educational equator, we say, and we need not reward them simply for what they ought to naturally be doing.

Again, we return to the idea of beginning with the end in mind. It is this premise that causes me to purchase all those pencils. In the end, what do I want for my students? I want them to do their classwork and to learn. If they lack the tools, time is wasted towards the end goal. It is too easy to assign the lack-of-a-pencil problem to the students alone. When someone in my class cannot reach the end goal for any reason, it becomes my problem, too. My solution is not enabling; it is cost effective, time effective, and wholly appropriate to the climate of motivation that I wish to engender in my classroom. Now, if I could only find a pair of matching socks. . . .

THE DESK NEXT TO THE TEACHER'S

There is not one face or one label that can be attached to the students who trudge both ways up the hill of education. The following vignettes are based upon the faces and stories of many students who have left footprints on my heart. Through them, the students call to us from all grade levels, all corners of the room, and all ability levels.

Everyone knows Johnny. He's the boy with the ready smile and twinkle of mischief who always has his desk pushed up next to the teacher's. On his best days, Johnny is animated and active and on his worst days, he's disruptive. He just can't seem to sit still. When the teacher talks with him about it, his eyes are sincere as he insists that he *wants* to behave but just doesn't know how. He promises to try harder and for a very short time, the whispering and the squirming and the throwing of his pencil in the air stop. His primary-grade teachers are captivated by Johnny's "Dennis the Menace" demeanor, sometimes in spite of themselves. His intermediate teachers like his enthusiasm and quick wit. They take extra care to send Johnny on errands to the office or to seek supplies from the custodian. They consciously give him time to stretch his limbs in ways that don't distract the other students.

Then, in middle school, Johnny's teachers only have him for forty-five minutes a day. They want him to stay in his seat. They want him to close his mouth. They need him to be an open vessel for the sake of the upcoming tests and for the sake of a controlled classroom atmosphere. Johnny tries hard to stay in his seat, he focuses his attention towards the board and tries to drown out the buzzing of the fluorescent lighting overhead and the voices that occasionally arise from the hall outside. On days when there is cooperative learning in the classroom, Johnny feels like a coiled spring that has suddenly been released. He leaps into action, bouncing his way around the classroom until he learns that group work, too, has physical boundaries.

By the time he gets to high school, Johnny drinks two cans of caffeinated soda before the school day begins. He finds that it helps him focus. He doesn't know why. In fact, Johnny has begun to wonder why he bothers to focus at all. School isn't much fun anymore. His teachers have long stopped finding him engaging or cute. He doesn't talk much to anyone and he is very tired of listening. The lights still make noise, the hallways still echo, and the teacher's voice becomes a muted chorus with them. Johnny is bored and worse than that, he's falling behind. There is more to learn and he has far less motivation to learn it. There is more to absorb and he has already reached the threshold of a student sponge. Johnny begins to wonder if school is really worth it, after all.

IF FEAR COULD WHISPER

Makayla shares her bedroom with two of her sisters and her five-year-old brother, who is too young to notice girls yet—at least, she hopes he is. They live in a cramped trailer about three miles from school. The intersection where the bus picks her up overwhelms her sometimes, with the honking of horns and the drivers who ignore the school zone signs. She is often afraid when she gets to school. She is first afraid of the big yellow bus as it swallows her. It is larger than her bedroom. She wonders if it is larger than her whole trailer. Next, she is afraid of the rude loud boys who sit in the back of the bus. Her little brother is afraid, too. He clings to her and tries to hold her hand but she won't let him. Life is hard enough when you are from another country and don't speak the language of your classmates very well. The raucous boys in the back of the bus call her names that make her face burn with embarrassment. The bus driver doesn't stop them and she wonders if it is because he, too, thinks that the names are true.

She would never admit it, but she is afraid of the hallways at her school, too. She struggles with the lock on her locker, her small fingers flexing again and again to conquer the puzzling combination. She liked it better in third grade, when she had a bright hook and a cubbyhole with her name spelled out in happy red crayon letters.

Makayla doesn't raise her hand in school. She has been in the U.S. for three years but still the language is unpredictable and fast and her accent is apparent. She tries to do the homework that is assigned in the quiet time that the teacher gives them but she is often confused. She's afraid, too, of asking questions. Sometimes, she tries to do her homework in her tiny bedroom, but her sisters fight and whine and her little brother makes all sorts of noises as he tries to build a city with his blocks. Usually, she turns in whatever work she has accomplished and prays that it is enough.

She gets in real trouble when the teacher calls home. The teacher has to use a translator and the words seem to come out cold and uncaring. She hears the warmth in her teacher's voice at school and knows that her teacher means no harm but her parents are embarrassed by the call. They shout at her and make her cry. Discipline is very different in her home country. She wishes she could tell the teacher not to call.

SIMPLE GIFTS?

Twelve-year-old Jamie likes it when his teachers make mistakes on the chalkboard. He is always the first to raise his hand and point out the error. He thinks it is especially amusing when his teacher says, "I meant to do that, I was testing you to see if you'd notice." He never smiles when his teachers say that because he knows it isn't true. His teachers always seem to make such simple mistakes. They give him easy work that he can get done well before the other students in the room.

At first, Jamie thought that it was cool to finish his work early. He liked having time to read or to draw pictures at his desk. He felt just a little bit smug when his teacher asked him to tutor other students. But the novelty of doing all those things wore off fairly quickly. He grew bored and restless, fidgeting in his seat and figuring out ways to get other kids in trouble without implicating himself. When he was in fourth grade, the school told his parents that his IQ made him eligible for a program for the gifted but that his disruptive behavior prevented him from receiving the service. In fifth grade, shortly after he found a way to access all of the teacher's computer files by figuring out her secret password, the school reconsidered and placed him in the program.

Once again, Jamie found himself vastly disappointed. The teacher was nice enough and he was glad that she didn't talk to him in that patronizing tone that so many other teachers used but she was only there once a week. She was more like a cheerleader than a teacher, he decided, always telling him that he was responsible for finding ways to challenge his brain. If that was the extent of her service, Jamie decided, then he wanted no part of it. He didn't like getting pulled out of the classroom to a separate room as if he were some sort of fifth-grade freak show anyway. Jamie stopped attending the program. Besides, he told himself, figuring out that password had certainly challenged his brain. . . .

YOU DON'T KNOW JACK

Misty looked at the crumpled shape of her father passed out on the kitchen floor and wondered if she had a split personality. Not half an hour ago, she had chaired a student council meeting. She had dropped off homework for a sick friend, picked up a few groceries on the way home from school, and had used her cell phone to make certain that her little brother remembered to go to piano practice. Now, she was in her own kitchen bent over her alcoholic father, checking to see if he was still breathing. She'd learned about alcohol poisoning in school. She wondered why the thought of coming home and finding him dead didn't bother her more. At least then it would be over.

She didn't know if she could juggle all the responsibility much longer. Her mother couldn't take it and had ventured off for parts unknown a few years ago. Things hadn't been too bad until then. When the recession hit and her father lost his job, they'd gotten much worse. Misty wondered if she should just put the pillow from his bed on the kitchen floor for him. She wondered if he'd understand the significance of that.

Mr. Turner, the guidance counselor, had talked with her that day at school. He'd used words like *potential* and *high achiever* but it hurt her to listen to him too closely. She was just so tired. She saw her father's bourbon glass on the counter. It was still half full. In a way, he looked so peaceful. She wondered what it would be like to not be tired. Misty picked up the glass.

STICKS AND STONES

It seemed to him that he had spent his whole life wishing that his name wasn't Rob. *Blob* rhymed with Rob. In second grade, he decided to do something about it. He decided that he wanted to be called Robert and insisted that everyone address him that way. He wouldn't answer them unless they did so. Then, the kids started calling him Blobert. He didn't like that, either.

He remembered the first time that he was aware, truly aware, that people were of all different sizes. He was on a field trip to the zoo with his preschool class. He was four years old, soon to enter kindergarten. He was sitting on the train next to his friend Derek as they passed the giraffes. Derek had giggled and said, "Hey, that looks like my mom." This brought a few small laughs and some fond smiles from the adult chaperones. Derek's mom was very tall and Derek's easy association was cute. It was not so cute, however, when they passed the elephants and Derek exclaimed, "And there's your mom!"

Derek's comment had been made in innocence but the kids were past the age of innocence now. They'd called him Blob for so long that he wondered if any of them remembered that he had a real name. They'd wished him off their playing fields, out of their clubs, and away from their social circles. His mother kept telling him to wait for high school when they would mature. He sat home alone first through homecoming and then through prom. Over the summer, he got a job doing data entry at his father's office. He liked the privacy of his cubicle. He liked the safety of the numbers and the consistency of the keyboard beneath his fingertips. The thought of three more years of school depressed him. He began to wonder if he could find work without a diploma. He didn't know if he could survive another lonely prom.

AND BABY MAKES TWO

She knew that she was supposed to feel guilty about being pregnant. All of her teachers gave her reproachful looks as she tried to squeeze herself into the uncompromising metal desks in their classrooms. She didn't really feel guilty, though. She liked sex. She hadn't liked it when she was eleven and Uncle Mark had come into her room and . . . but wait, she was not supposed to talk about that. Her mother had said that that was just the way with some men. Uncle Dwayne had proved her right. But after all that, when she learned that she could be in control and dole it out to the eager boys in her class like candy, she had learned to like it. She liked the feeling of power. She liked babies, too. It was important to have people to love you in the world and she was simply starting early. Her baby would love her, too. She smiled to herself as she pictured a quietly cooing pink bundle of baby powder joy.

THE FACES OF STRUGGLE

The faces of the students who struggle in school are as broad as the characterizations you've just read. They are of all ages, all races, and all intellectual and socioeconomic levels. More significantly, they are of all learning styles, bringing a broad spectrum of gifts and talents to the classroom. When I sat down to try to bring to life the qualities of the students in my classroom, I found my poetic side. When I finished sharing this poem with my group of eighth graders, there was a hushed silence in the room. They were touched and appreciative. Sometimes, it's difficult to take emotional risks with students. With any risk, there is a fear of rejection, of ridicule, or of failure to communicate a true intention. The appreciative smiles of the students, however, make it well worth the risk.

The Gifts
Sometimes you are a whirlwind.
Scattering papers, forgetting your pencil
Doodling the chalkboard full before I can stop you
Your voice is a bellow
You tap your pencil in time with your toes
And still you know when it is your turn to read.
You give the gift of energy.

Sometimes you are quiet.
Ducking your head, hiding your face
Cradling your emotions in the crook of your arm

You refuse to work
You look as if you want to cry but you don't
And still you learn the times tables.
You give the gift of reflection.

Sometimes you are the town crier.
Blurting your feelings, telling the truth
Whispering in my ear that Paul didn't get breakfast
That Jenny gets hit
That Samuel's mom drinks beer
You are always on the edge of someone's secret.
You give the gift of observation.

Sometimes, the classroom is your stage.
Mimicking the teacher, making faces
Giggling at the sounds of your own body
Your cheeks turn red with laughter
You prove to us that school can be fun
And sometimes you don't get your spelling done.
You give the gift of humor.

Sometimes, your heart is on your sleeve.
Passing out papers, leading the line
Smiling at the new girl in the back row
Even though she doesn't smile back.
You share your peanut butter with Jared
You tell me that he didn't have time to pack a lunch.
You give the gift of kindness.

CHAPTER TWO

CREATING CLIMATE

*Strategies for Building Relationships, Encouraging Risk
Taking, and Revitalizing Curriculum*

THE GOLDEN RULES

When my son was ten, we were celebrating the fourth of July
at a local park. At dusk, we positioned ourselves at a grassy
spot along the man-made lake that was in the center of the
park because it was a good vantage point for watching the
fireworks. It was a hot evening and a few teenagers near us
decided to take advantage of the lake. They began jumping
off the nearby dock, splashing and yelling in their enjoy-
ment of the adventure. Of course, my son wanted to do the
same. Since this was typically not a lake for swimming, I told
him he could not go in the water. He asked me, "Why not?"
and I told him that the lake really wasn't made for swimming. He pointed out that there was no sign to indicate this.
My response was to affirm that the park simply expected
people to know this because the purpose of the lake was for
aesthetic pleasure. He sat back on the blanket and sighed
deeply. "I guess that is just another one of life's many unwritten rules, hm?"

Life is full of unwritten rules. Most children seem to
learn them through a combination of home, school and
community education, and osmosis. Students who struggle

in school, however, often don't learn them at the same rate or in the same manner as their peers.

I will never forget six-year-old Devin, who had the combined energy of at least ten wriggling earthworms. He used to navigate my classroom "as the crow flies," jumping over or walking across the tops of any furniture in his path. One day, having redirected him yet again on going around the table-top instead of over it, I asked him, "Do you climb over the tops of your tables at home?" He seemed surprised at the question, quickly affirming that he did, indeed, play leap-frog with his household furnishings with wild abandon.

Leanne couldn't seem to control her anger in school. She was highly disruptive in class, frequently cursed at her peers and her teachers, and got in several verbal altercations. Phone conversations and meetings with her mother had been unsuccessful but were necessary each time that disciplinary action was taken. It was during one such call that her mother asked me if I had a calendar. Affirming that I did, she told me, "Mark today's date on your calendar. I have PMS. Check every month before you call and NEVER call me when I have PMS." With that, my ear met the dial tone.

One of the greatest fallacies in our schools is that students will have garnered all of the appropriate school behaviors that they require before they cross the educational equator. Most students have already been in school for four years. They have heard countless admonitions to raise their hands, stay in their seats, and not talk to their neighbors. Their teachers have made numerous attempts to mold the behaviors that are necessary to create a climate of learning within a classroom. When some children persist in blurting out answers, moving about the room at will, and whispering to the child in the next desk, teachers get frustrated. Shaping behaviors rapidly turn to blaming behaviors and students find themselves in trouble again and again and again.

It is a vicious cycle. When students have not attained the personal skills necessary to learn the social skills that exist on the other side of the educational equator, they lag behind with a deficit that will ultimately make them a victim of the educational system. When students cross the academic equator with reading difficulties or deficits in math, there are a host of school programs designed to help them achieve success. Academic deficits are remediated because academics are what is measured on standardized tests. Behavioral deficits, however, are judged with an increasingly severe system of "oughts." Students receive the messages of "You ought to know better." "You ought to have learned that in first grade." "You ought to act your age." "You ought to be more responsible," "less disruptive," "more mature." Is there a quicker way to create disillusionment than to demand what may be impossible or improbable? Teachers often find interpersonal learners disruptive because they rely on conversing with other students to enhance learning. Kinesthetic learners are frustrating because of their need to be out of their seats. Students with musical or intrapersonal intelligence may seem as though they are daydreaming as they try to reframe what they are learning into something more meaningful to their learning style. Students' early school years are filled with song and movement in a very tactile environment. Pictures make textbooks highly visual. Teachers read aloud, providing for a student's auditory needs. In short, students on the primary side of the educational equator often do not reflect at-risk learning characteristics simply because their instructional environment is suited to their learning style. Why then, when they cross over to the intermediate side of the equator, do they become "at-risk"? Isn't it their educational environment that is a risk to them?

THE THREE R'S

Creating a positive classroom climate is the most important role that any teacher has. It's all about Relationship, Relationship, and Relationship. Relationships between teachers and students are typically built in three different ways. First, there is the development of student-focused relationships. Under this model, educators work to get to know each student personally. They interact with students on a familiar level on subjects outside of the curriculum. They strive to get students to know each other and to appreciate the unique gifts that others bring to the classroom setting. Teachers who endeavor to form student-focused relationships enjoy cooperative learning activities. They facilitate classroom discussions that allow students to fully participate by making all answers acceptable and safe. They both model and teach the skills of tolerance and acceptance of diversity to their students.

Second, there are teacher-focused relationships. Teachers share freely about their personal lives, decorate the classrooms to reflect their personal beliefs and tastes, and use many stories in their lessons with students. In this model, the teacher sees herself as the purveyor of knowledge. She strives to engage students through familiarity. She puts them at ease through her openness. Students are encouraged to share by her example but they are not pressured. Teacher-focused relationship building allows students to unfold at an individual pace.

Finally, there are academics-focused relationships. In this platform, classrooms are primarily focused on academics. Teachers evidence an enthusiasm for children, for employing a vast array of learning strategies, and for engaging all learners. These educators are passionate about the subject matter that they are teaching and they expect that their learners will be passionate, too. Relationships are developed centering around success with curriculum. It is critical that teachers individualize instructional strategies because it is the ability to master the curriculum that affords the relationship to the student.

Many teachers effectively infuse values from all three relationship models into their classrooms. What is most important to remember is that relationship building is both an active and a cognitive process. It is active because teachers must constantly attempt to find ways to engross all learners and it is cognitive because they must also engage in ongoing professional development activities to acquire the skills to reach an increasingly diverse student body.

There are many ways to build relationships with students. There are Internet sources, books, and seminars dedicated to strategies to captivate all learners. It is vital that educators find the shoes that fit best. I am primarily a student-focused relationship builder. Throughout this book, I will offer my favorite activities in any given area. I hope they will be as productive and as comfortable for you as they are for me. However, if they are not a match for your unique style, I encourage you to use any of the resources found in Appendix A. Strategies for relationship building are found on page 24.

SAILING THE THREE C'S OF CLIMATE

The American Heritage Dictionary describes climate as "A prevailing condition or set of attitudes in human affairs."[1] It can be surmised, then, that classroom climate is the set of attitudes that predominates between students and teachers and students with peers. It is always the classroom teachers' responsibility to establish a climate suitable for both learning and growing. Climate is not dependent on the mix of students one has, the amount of curriculum that one has to squeeze in, or the support (or lack thereof) of the parents, school administration, or community. It is irresponsible for a classroom teacher to ever claim a victim status with regard to the formation of a positive classroom climate. There are no excuses. The *Dimensions of Learning* model[2] for classroom instruction views climate as of ultimate importance. The very first component of this model states that at its most basic level, learning is dependent upon students' attitudes about school, the material to be learned, and their own ability to affect learning both positively and negatively.

A multitude of components affects relationship building in a classroom. In this chapter, we will examine three critical

WAYS TO BUILD RELATIONSHIPS AMONG STUDENTS

Suits Me

Each group is given part of a deck of cards. Via "luck of the draw" each member must share the following, depending on which card they draw:

- Hearts: One of their favorite activities and why it is a favorite
- Diamonds: One of their favorite restaurants or foods and why it is a favorite
- Spades: One of their favorite sports and why it is a favorite
- Clubs: One of their favorite songs and why it is a favorite

Growing Teams

Each team is given the parts for a flower (center, petals, stem, leaves). As a team, they must determine something that all have in common and write it in the center. Each person should determine something unique they bring and put it on a petal, attaching it as they share. As a team, all should decide one thing that makes them all feel supported and write it on the stem. Each person should write a trait that would make them wish a person would leave the group and write it on a leaf.

Quotes That Define

Each person is given a list of quotes that the teacher feels are age appropriate. Many quotes can be found in books, calendars, or on the Internet. Each student should choose the quote that best matches his or her personality and be prepared to share it with the group.

Feelings Check-in

Pass out markers and 5 × 8 index cards. Ask each student to write on the card in large letters one word that describes how he or she is feeling right now. Then ask

24

students to hold up their cards and look at the variety of responses. Point out how rare it is for different people to bring the same feelings to an experience or situation. Invite students to share why they wrote down the words that they did. A variation on this would be to present situations to children and ask them to hold up pre-made cards indicating how involvement in that situation would make them feel.

Popcorn

One student (or the teacher) should begin to share personal statistics (e.g., "I have one cat") favorite things (e.g., "I like pizza"). When someone else in the room can relate to one of those favorite things (i.e., "I like pizza, too") they should "pop up" and wait for the person speaking to call on them. The person who pops up then begins to share more things, waiting for someone else to pop up with another commonality.

"C's" of climate: Communication, Courage, and Curriculum. Individually, each of these areas is vital toward building a structure of interdependence necessary for true learning. When combined together, they serve as a solid foundation supporting the development of lifelong learning.

'TWAS BRILLIG, AND THE SLITHY TOVES

During my first year of teaching, I worked with students with emotional and learning disabilities in a small rural middle school. When my very first parent-teacher conference time rolled around, I was nervous. Would I know what to say? Would the parents like me? Would I make a good impression? Conferences were not individually scheduled and parents were free to drop into my classroom anytime during the evening. I was poised at my table with an eager smile, sharpened pencils, and individual portfolios of all my students' work. When the first parent walked through my classroom door, I was as prepared as I could possibly be. And then she spoke. "I don't know what the [expletive] you [expletive] people think you're doing but I don't know why my [expletive] kid's always in trouble." My smile faded but I held out my hand and tried to be gracious. "You must be Jason's mom," I said, and I invited her to sit down. To this day, I wonder why she never asked how it was that I knew that she was Jason's mom. Perhaps it is because she knew that their vocabularies were so very much alike.

Communication is vital to the establishment and maintenance of classroom climate. Communication is both innate and learned. Human beings have an innate interdependence that is fostered by quality communication. Thus, possessing good communication skills is critical to the creation of a positive learning environment. However, the development of good communication skills is *not* innate. Instead, children pick up on whatever tools are around them and use those tools to frame their own interactions. Jason's communication reflected his mother's. The communication style used in Jason's home was so dominating that he had never internalized other ways to express himself. It was the same with Leticia. Leticia could have been wearing a business suit when she walked into my office to enroll in our school. Formal attire would have reflected the professional calm that she exuded. Her mother had sent her into the building to pick up whatever forms were required to admit her into school and Leticia had taken it upon herself to set up an impromptu meeting with the principal, too. I smiled at her and she didn't return the smile. Instead, she began to look testy and drum her short red fingernails on the tabletop in a mimic of impatience. She looked me straight in the eye and said, "I think you should know that school is a waste of time and that I plan to drop out as soon as I can." Only then did she smile sweetly, turn on her heel, and stride purposefully out of my office.

One of the first steps to teaching positive communications skills to students is to model them. The best prescription for communication that I have found is simple. Stop. Look. Listen. Respond. It is important that even though there is one more paper to correct, one more plant to water, or one more art project to clean up, a teacher stops to listen. It is also important to make eye contact. Then, active listening can take place. Active listening involves concentrated listening, asking appropriate questions, and interjecting comments that demonstrate understanding. In other words, respond. Active listening is not only a powerful way to model good communication skills, it is also an excellent way to show caring for a student.

CAN YOU HEAR WHAT I'M SEEING?

"Oh, the comfort, the inexplicable comfort of feeling safe with a person, having neither to weigh thought nor measure words, but to pour them all out just as they are, chaff and grain together, knowing your friend, with the breath of kindness, will blow the chaff away." I've had these beautiful words by George Eliot posted by my desk for as long as I can recall. Students of all ages benefit from unconditional listening; for students who struggle in school, it is critical. Unconditional listening is best defined as "listening without judgment or correction." For example, when one of my students is sharing a story about her weekend and she says, "And I seen the coolest jeans at the mall," I need to listen without interruption and save the grammar lesson for another time. Students who are consistently corrected for their normal patterns of speech soon don't have the desire to share their stories. And their stories are essential to building a classroom climate. When another student shares his experience of being at a bar with his dad and his uncles until two o'clock in the morning and of drinking beer with them, as an unconditional listener it is my job only to hear his story and not to add my personal value judgment to it. I might ask, "How did you feel about that?" or I might simply ask a benign question such as, "How many uncles do you have?" to show that I am listening. The time for adding personal value judgments is well after a relationship has been built and trust between the speaker and the listener is firmly established.

I've noticed over the years that students who struggle in school and especially those deemed "at-risk" in their educational environments have some receptive language barriers that augment their difficulties in school. The crux of the dysfunction is that they do not seem to readily understand generalized speech. I often refer to it as the "ego phenomenon." At-risk students miss many directions, lecture notes, and announcements because they simply do not tune in to any matter that does not seem to directly be about them. In the classroom, this is most easily solved by walking by their desks and giving a brief tap, making consistent eye contact, or by saying their names aloud. Beyond that, though, a teacher can also discuss a verbal "cue" with a student and teach him to respond to generalized terms. Consider the example of Thao. Thao never seemed to hear the teacher when she gave directions. Immediately after the other students had begun to work, he would still be sitting at his desk, looking confused. At first, his teacher would walk by his desk and tap his paper, saying "Get started." Still Thao sat there, unmoving and unspeaking. He was afraid to tell the teacher that he hadn't heard the directions. In the past, his teachers had scolded him for refusing to pay attention. However, Thao tried hard to pay attention. Sometimes, though, it was as if the directions got lost in the large mix of words that his teacher was using. It turned out that Thao knew *how* to listen but that he didn't really know *when* to listen. Once his teacher realized this, she was able to give him the cue of the word *class*. She told Thao that whenever she used the word *class*, that she was about to give an assignment and that he should prepare to write that assignment down.

Other students seem to know when to listen but they don't seem to really grasp how to personalize the directions so that they are able to get started on an assignment. Asking these children to repeat the directions for the group, write them on the board, or write them immediately in an agenda helps greatly.

Still other students do not know how or when to listen. Often, teachers assume that these are deliberate misbehaviors. Sometimes these students can be assigned a "study buddy" who quietly tunes them into what is happening in class. "Ear training" helps students, too. Teachers can outline lessons ahead of time and give a student a specific thing to listen for, such as, "John, I want you to listen for the name of the general who led American troops in World War II." The teacher can further cue John by saying, "And watch my face, because I am going to raise my eyebrows just before I share that information."

The evolution from egocentric to more group-focused learning occurs naturally for most students on the primary side of the educational equator. Most, however, is not all. It is harmful for teachers to assume that a student's receptive and expressive language skills are normal simply because the student doesn't receive special services. When in doubt, teach and reteach. Students who can develop the skills of good communication will ultimately have less struggle in school and in life.

ONE DAY MORE

While commanding troops during World War II, General George Patton was quoted as saying, "Courage is fear holding on one minute longer." Mahatma Gandhi said, "Courage has never been known to be a matter of muscle; it is a matter of the heart. The toughest muscle has been known to tremble before an imaginary fear. It was the heart that set the muscle atrembling." In *None of Our Business*, I dedicated an entire chapter to many factors that cause inequities and subsequent fear in the educational system. Parker Palmer, author of *The Courage to Teach* (1998), has written extensively about the courage that is present each day in our public schools.

ACTIVITIES TO TEACH AND ENHANCE COMMUNICATION SKILLS

Life With the Wright Family[3]

Have the class sit or stand in a circle and give them each a paperclip. As you read the story of "Life With the Wright Family" (Appendix B), they need to pass the paperclip to the right every time they hear the word "right" or "Wright" and to the left each time they hear the word "left." Start reading the story slowly so they have a chance to catch on and gradually pick up speed. Stop a few times during the story to see how they are doing and if they each have one object still or if a few folks have accumulated three or four. After the activity, have a discussion about how activity affects story comprehension, how tension affects listening, and how extraneous activity makes it difficult to pay attention, and about how focusing on one communication goal (passing the clips) changes the value of another communication goal (hearing the story).

Worst and Best

This was one of my elementary students' favorite activities at the start of each day. After fifth grade, students seem to prefer to have this sort of communication more privately in a "teacher-response" journal.

While seated in a circle, students share first the worst and then the best things that have happened to them in the last day. Students will learn to vocalize their feelings and frustrations in a positive way and at the same time they will learn to be better listeners. Students will also get to know one another better and then will hopefully be more supportive of one another. Starting with the worst and ending with the best allows things to end on a positive note.

Think-Pair-Share[4]

1. Think. The teacher provokes students' thinking with a question or prompt or observation. The students should take a few moments (probably not minutes) just to THINK about the question.

2. Pair. Using designated partners, students PAIR up to talk about the answer each came up with. They compare their mental or written notes and identify the answers they think are best, most convincing, or most unique.

3. Share. After students talk in pairs for a few moments, the teacher calls for pairs to SHARE their thinking with the rest of the class. She can do this by going around in round-robin fashion, calling on each pair; or she can take answers as they are called out (or as hands are raised). Often, the teacher or a designated helper will record these responses on the board or on the overhead.

Learning Chain

This is a variation of the traditional "I'm going on a trip" game and can be used in any subject area.

The first player says, "I'm a valuable part of (subject) class and something we've learned is _____." The player then names a new concept or idea. The second player then says, "I'm a valuable part of (subject) class and some things we've learned are _____ and _____." The player repeats the first player's concept and then adds his own. This continues among however many participants the teacher decides should be a part of each circle.

Building a Peanut Butter and Jelly Sandwich Through Communication[5]

Ask for one volunteer to be a computer robot. The robot can do only as it is instructed. Have the robot temporarily leave the room so they do not hear you explain the task to the other students. Explain to the group that you want the robot to do a very simple task: successfully make a peanut butter and jelly sandwich. Place the jar of peanut butter, jelly, knife, and bread on a table and invite the robot back into the room. Ask one volunteer to suggest the first step. For example, a student says,

"Put the peanut butter on the bread." The robot should do exactly this: place the peanut butter jar on the loaf or slice of bread. Continue to ask for suggestions from the students. Each time, the robot should do exactly as instructed. If an instruction is too vague, the robot can ask for another, more specific instruction (or hold up an error message). Remind students to speak one at a time, and encourage lots of participation. Eventually, with lots of trial and error, the robot should end up with a peanut butter and jelly sandwich. Discuss how communication can be misinterpreted, how what is omitted from a message can change meaning, and how a dialogue versus a directive promotes understanding.

What is it about the intangible quality of courage that contributes so significantly to a classroom that it is ranked among the three vital areas of climate? It is the fact that, as Parker Palmer says, "We teach who we are."[6] In fact, I would expand on Palmer's thought and add, "We learn who we are." Both phrases refer to living one's truth—of being a complete and genuine human being across all environments. This is what a good teacher wants for his students and this is what he must model. Palmer speaks about the courage that it takes to rid oneself of the negative baggage that inhibits an individual from becoming "whole." I am reminded of the scene in the movie *The NeverEnding Story*, in which Atreyu comes to a wall where all the brave knights who went before him have perished. It is the point of truth and self-knowledge and to cross the divide successfully, he must look at himself as he truly is.

In the best of circumstances, teaching is an exercise in vulnerability crafted into art. In the worst of circumstances, teaching is an exercise in vulnerability melted into failure. How a teacher handles either of the extremes speaks to her character and to her heart. Palmer says, "We became teachers for reasons of the heart, animated by a passion for some subject and for helping people to learn . . . The courage to teach is the courage to keep one's heart open in those very moments when the heart is asked to hold more than it is able, so that the teacher and students and subject can be woven into the fabric of community that learning and living require."[7]

In a speech given in 1999 to graduates in a teacher certification program, Michael Loui, a professor of electrical and computer engineering, acknowledges that classroom courage is not limited to instructors.

> We teachers are not the only ones who need courage in the classroom. In order to learn, students also need courage to overcome their fears. Courage to engage in a discussion that challenges their deepest convictions about racial bias or global warming or technological progress or architectural aesthetics. Courage to ask questions that may reveal their ignorance. Courage to prepare for a final examination with problems they do not know in advance on subjects they do not understand completely. Courage to take risks to learn new concepts and skills.[8]

Research shows us that children have worries and that they bring those concerns with them each day to the classroom. For some, the worries are about friendships and academics. For others, the anxieties are about health, family issues such as money and stress, and fear and intimidation in their school environments. Still others are stressed by the stark realities of homelessness, drug use, domestic and sexual abuse, and hunger. To this end, *we learn who we are.* It is critical for educators to understand that when Jillian looks out the window, doodles in her notebook, and doesn't open her textbook that she is thinking about the rough feel of her father's hands in the middle of the night. It is important to have empathy for the fact that when Gerald doesn't stay seated it is because the hard wood of the desk makes his bruised body ache. When Lydia is afraid that Jolene is going to take her lunch for the third day in a row, the math lesson becomes secondary to her growing concern. It takes courage to know who our students really are but genuine learning cannot take place until we do.

It takes courage from both students and teachers to grow in these times of educational injustice. The sanctions imposed by the No Child Left Behind plan create a devastating learning environment, especially for those schools that are already overwhelmed by inequitable social conditions. Fear and shame about testing are anathema to the goals of learning. When writing about listening to the teacher within, Palmer makes a strong statement against a system of education driven by disconnected and arbitrary forces. He writes, "When I follow only the oughts, I may find myself doing work that is essentially laudable but that is not mine to do. A vocation that is not mine, no matter how externally valued, does violence to the self—in the precise sense that it violates my identity and integrity on behalf of some abstract norm. When I violate myself, I invariably end up violating the people that I work with. How many teachers inflict their own pain on their students—the pain that comes from doing a work that never was, or no longer is, their true work?"[9]

OH, THE PLACES YOU'LL GO . . . EVENTUALLY

For students who struggle in school, the curriculum is often the enemy. They ask, with derision, "When am I going to use this in the real world?" They whine that the lessons are boring and stupid. They make faces, rest their heads upon their desks, or poke at the student in the next desk just to prove that they do not share their teacher's goals.

Educators do themselves a great disservice by trying to justify their curriculum. As a teacher of students with behavioral disabilities, I did classroom observations whenever a referral was made to the emotional disabilities (ED) program. It was on one such visit that I heard the familiar query about the usefulness of learning to add fractions. Becky's

ACTIVITIES TO ENHANCE COURAGE AND RISK-TAKING

Courage in Action

In this activity, students are encouraged to portray their own definitions of courage. Using digital cameras, students go on an exploratory mission within their schools to find and photograph examples of "courage in action." Later, they download their photos and write or give a speech about why the picture represents courage. This activity can be done in groups or individually. A modification would be to create a "courage collage" using pictures from magazines.

Courage in the Press

In this activity, students use newspapers and magazines to gather articles that detail the traits of courageous individuals. Students then share the results of their searches with one another. The teacher can facilitate discussion by creating a "looks like, sounds like" chart that accompanies the character traits that students have uncovered in their investigations.

The Face of Courage

Students create masks that detail the "faces" of courage. The teacher can encourage risk-taking in the classroom by reminding students that they all have faces of courage that they are able to pull out and use. Further discussion can center around hiding behind a mask of courage versus a mask of despair (or any other trait that the educator wishes to compare with courage).

Risk Pads[10]

Give each of your students a pad of paper labeled as a "Risk Pad." After teaching a new concept, put a sample problem on the board, ask your students to get out their Risk Pads, and challenge them with a directive such as: "Take a risk with this one. Work it out on your Risk Pads. Let us see what we can learn from our risk." Through

the use of special pads with a special name, you legiti-
mize risk-taking and the acceptance of challenges in
your classroom.

Mistake Coupons

At the beginning of each quarter, students are given
three "mistake coupons" with the expectation that they
are to use them before the next grading period begins.
Mistake coupons can be used for homework forgetfulness, misbehavior in class (with the exception of physical violence), or to remove grades from an assignment
that was done poorly. There should be a place on the
back of the coupon to write the new learning that
resulted from the mistake. It is helpful to explain the
motto "Mistakes don't become problems until you refuse
to correct them" to the class and to place it somewhere
on the mistake coupon. This activity allows students to
view the learning environment as flexible, encourages
them to think about risk-taking, and invites them to
make peaceable amends for mistakes they've made.

hand shot up as she challenged her teacher. Her teacher's
response was, "Well, think of baking a cake. You'd use fractions to double the recipe." Not to be subdued, Becky
frowned and thought for a moment. Then her hand shot
into the air as she asked, "Well, couldn't I just add the ingre-
dients twice each?"

The look that the teacher gave Becky was smoldering
and the look that she gave to me was significant. "See?" it
said, "Becky really does have behavioral issues."

So how should a teacher address the age-old question of
curricular utility? Honest answers work best. My reply to the
oft-asked "When am I going to use this?" is, "You are probably never going to use this particular skill in the real world."
The students are stunned. The next question is inevitably
"Then why do I have to learn it?"

I explain to my students that learning is very different from skill acquisition. During the process of solving multi-step equations, they are learning the life skills of organization, sequence, structure, and patience. They are learning that the answer doesn't always come easily, that applying a pattern to their lives will often allow them to garner predictable results, and that adherence to a structured set of rules sometimes breeds greater success than a pell-mell approach to any situation.

When students tell me that a lesson is boring, I sometimes agree with them. I teach five subjects a day and I don't love them all. I've never enjoyed science. Placing jazzy window dressings on the chemical properties of malleable metals neither entertains me nor inspires me to learn. Sometimes when a student says a lesson is boring, they mean that it is painful to them. As an example, I think about having to sew on a button. I hate to sew. I'm not good at it and even the thought of a simple button makes my fingers clench in dismay. I know even before I begin that the eye of the needle won't cooperate, that the button will shift and struggle beneath my fingertips, and that there will be an inexplicable residual bulge of thread on my material when I am finished. Sewing is a painful process to me even before I engage in it. It is easier to call it boring or meaningless.

When students complain about a lesson, it is a good time to teach sensitivity. It cannot be assumed that children know when they are being rude or hurting feelings. They need to learn that not only do they not need to share *everything* that they're thinking, but also that when they feel compelled to share, there are constructive and helpful ways to give feedback. A typical teacher dialogue might go something like this.

ANTWON: I hate this. It's so boring!

TEACHER: Math was never my favorite subject, either. What do you suppose my goal was when I dreamed up this lesson?

ANTWON: I dunno.

TEACHER: Well, my goal was to get you the information in the best way possible. It's my job to help you learn things and I like my job. Do you agree that it probably wasn't my goal to make you feel bored?

ANTWON: I guess.

TEACHER: Well, you're right. And frankly, it's kind of rude to tell me that my lessons bore you . . . especially because I try to make them interesting for you because I care about you. Do you know what I wish you'd do instead of just telling me it's boring?

ANTWON: What?

TEACHER: I wish that you'd find a part you liked and comment on that. Then, I wish that you'd tell me one thing that I could do to make it more appealing to you. In fact, class, that's exactly how we give what is called constructive criticism. . . .

The teacher can then elaborate on the components of constructive criticism and ask the class to practice aloud or in a journal. Making a student's behavior a teachable moment and not a preachable moment does much to assist with classroom management, climate, and acceptance of curriculum.

SADDLE UP YOUR LEAR JET

Knowledge is all around us all the time. One startling claim is that the average worker today receives more information in a day than the average worker in 1900 did in a lifetime. What's more, typical workers get an interruption every eight minutes, and that interruption takes an average of five minutes.[11] Why then, do we insist on taking away the tools of technology from students in the name of learning? Why do we ask them to sit in quiet rows as we frown over the slightest interruption?

I feel the urge to look over my shoulder for Susan Ohanian's legendary standardistos as I type this . . . but . . . I let my students use calculators in math. There are calculators today that sort fractions and negative numbers, perform orders of operations with ease, and that even understand why mathematical problems have parentheses in them. Of course students need to understand the principles behind the solution, but it is equally important for them to understand how to access and use the technology that will allow them to keep pace in the workforce. This may shock my high school math teachers, but I have never used an algebraic equation or a geometrical theorem in my adult life. And if I suddenly found myself immersed in them for some unfathomable reason, I would hurry to the nearest office supply store and get a twenty-dollar calculator.

With more to learn in less time, students need to learn to use the tools that will be at their disposal as adults. I sometimes think that adults confuse the struggle to learn with actual learning. For example, I remember banging away on the keys of a typewriter for hours only to find that I had used the wrong version of American Psychological Association (APA) format for a college report. With sweat on my brow and a clench in my jaw, I rolled another piece of paper into the typewriter to correct the error of my ways. Was that struggle really called "learning"? Or was it merely exertion during the engagement of one of the lowest learning models—rote copying?

This discussion came up at our school. I was excited to share with my fellow language arts teachers that there were tools on the Web that would assist our students with the tedious act of building a bibliography. The tool simply asked that the information be filled in and it would then convert it to APA style. The unified response was, "Absolutely not. They need to learn APA style." I was puzzled; all of the students had already had a computer class during which they copied the format of a research paper. Included in that paper was a long bibliography. They were not allowed to use any shortcuts. It seemed to me if learning were the goal, they had then already "learned."

I raised this point but the group was adamant. "They need to learn APA style. They use it in high school." Couldn't they use the tool in high school, too? I wondered aloud and was met by disapproving frowns. "They need it in college," I was told. I protested that not all colleges even used APA style and certainly that any student bright enough for college could copy an existing format from one of the hundreds of books dedicated to the subject. "This is the way we teach it," I was told.

There is an old adage that states, "If you always do what you've always done, you'll always get what you've always gotten." In education, we've long known that rote memorization and lower-level thinking skills disenfranchise a large group of learners. Yet we continue to frustrate students and compel them to boredom, misbehavior, apathy, and disenchantment. The labor force's number-one plea is that schools produce problem solvers who can work together and who are well-versed in technology. The maxim cited above, combined with Will Rogers' wisdom, tells it like it is. Rogers said, "Even if you're on the right track, you'll get run over if you just sit there." When students are forced to sit in silence sweating over the details of design, they are not really learning. They are merely waiting to get run over.

CHAPTER THREE

CREATING CHARACTER

Practices That Focus on Classroom Management,
Character Education, Cooperative Learning,
and the Multiple Intelligences

MY WAY OR THE HIGHWAY

There's a story about a distraught woman standing by the driver's side of her car in a busy parking lot. She is frantically tugging at the locked car door, to no avail. Her keys hang idle in the ignition. A kind passer-by notices her difficulty and offers her a cell phone to call a locksmith. Miserable, the teary woman shares that she will be late for a very important job interview. Just as she is about to hit "send" on the cell phone, the passer-by smiles and makes her way to the passenger side of the car, opening the unlocked door with a flourish. Wiping her tears, the woman thanks the stranger and hurriedly remedies her problem and drives happily off to her job interview.

• Public education needs to look beyond the obvious in order to thrive.

• Fred Kofman and Peter Senge (1995) have done extensive research in the area of organizational leadership. In an article about getting to the heart of learning organizations, they profess that "Building learning organizations,

41

we are discovering, requires basic shifts in how we think and interact." Kofman and Senge go on to ask, "Why do we confront learning opportunities with fear rather than wonder? Why do we derive our self-esteem from knowing as opposed to learning? Why do we criticize before we even understand? Why do we create controlling bureaucracies when we attempt to form visionary enterprises? And why do we persist in fragmentation and piecemeal analysis as the world becomes more and more interconnected?"[1]

The current educational climate within the United States perpetuates the types of quandaries inherent in those questions. High-stakes assessments produce fear. Sanctions related to test scores pave the way for the destruction of wonder as rote learning of disconnected facts becomes the new educational barometer. Schools with inequitable conditions are given a public "report card" that addresses only the losses incurred and not the gains being made within that school's walls. The No One is Left Behind the Child Act provides the freedom to do as commanded, which is really no freedom at all. In an interconnected world, our legislators and our policy makers condone standards that stratify, comparisons that create educational caste systems, and assessments that are dangerously divisive.

THE CRITICAL FOURTH "C"

Three elements essential to a positive classroom climate were identified in Chapter 2. Classroom management is the critical fourth "C" of climate. Classroom management, however, is individual and not prescriptive. When a teacher truly builds a relationship with her students, she begins to manage her classroom as a series of individual personalities to be reckoned with rather than a set of factors to be controlled. There are, however, strategies that accompany fundamental principles of learning that encourage the development of sound classroom management practices.

Kofman and Senge identify three areas of current practice as "frozen patterns of thought to be dissolved"—fragmentation, competition, and reactiveness. They offer that our enchantment with fragmentation starts in early childhood. Since our first school days, we learn to break the world apart and disconnect ourselves from it. We memorize isolated facts, read static accounts of history, study abstract theories, and acquire ideas unrelated to our life experience and personal aspirations.[2]

Students who struggle in school are more negatively affected by fragmented learning systems than many of their peers. Often, at-risk students have a high degree of fragmentation in their home and social lives. There has been little consistency of thought in their parenting and in their relationship building. They are often seen as aimless drifters who graft themselves to the fad of the moment, the group with the most radical viewpoints, or to the predictable effects that chemicals will have upon their bodies. For these students, school does not provide the critical "grounding" that is necessary for learning. Often, these students see school as a series of unrelated smoke-and-mirrors acts. From the primary grades forward, they do not see the "whole" of the educational environment and subsequently do not have a personal buy-in to the eventual attainment of a high school diploma. As they progress through the grades, they become tired of jumping through the hoops of learning and they simply stop doing so.

Providing fluidity for students in an otherwise fragmented academic world is a key factor in managing behavior within a classroom. In a fluid classroom, learners have access to all of the tools needed for learning. Each learner has some small space to call his own. Learners are taught interdependence and caring for one another. The furniture is fluid, too, moving at will and adapting to the needs of the students. The teacher is fluid, being seemingly everywhere at once, able to move freely from student to student and rarely needing to turn his back on anyone. There is a structured balance between chaos and rigidity and an emphasis on blending self-expression and group goals. Students, teachers, and visitors are made to feel as though they are an essential living part of a work in progress.

Having been trained as a special education teacher and as a behaviorist, I didn't always believe in fluidity. In fact, at times I still struggle, sometimes suppressing and sometimes expressing a desire to put the students' desks in rows and to harangue them to remove their personal effects from the classroom. When I do decide on rows, it is because I feel us moving more towards chaos. When I sense a paralysis of learning because our environment has become too traditional, we move again into groups. As with any environment, there are students who keep their books and notebooks in neat rows in their lockers and students who slam their locker doors quickly in hope that nothing falls out. Within the classroom, there are students who are annoyed when the bookshelf becomes cluttered and others who don't even know that there *is* a bookshelf behind the clutter. The baskets beneath the desks in my classroom range from spartan space savers to hosts of an array of student projects that quite possibly date back to a child's kindergarten year.

Fluidity is governed by intuition. It is flavored by language. I have tried to phase out the words "my classroom" from my vocabulary and to replace them with "our classroom." When I return the students to rows, it is because *we* need the structure and the grounding that sitting in rows provides. When I speak to educators who share my students, I try to say "our students." Being proprietary not only segregates students in the minds of others, it also further fragments those students as learners.

Fluidity is also rooted in a firm belief of unconditional respect. Only when we respect others for who they are can we hope to make them better than where they are. Kofman and

Senge affirm that learning organizations must be grounded in three foundations:

1. a culture based on transcendent human values of love, wonder, humility, and compassion
2. a set of practices for generative conversation and coordinated action
3. a capacity to see and work with the flow of life as a system.

They maintain that a fragmented system of learning is transactional. The problem with a transactional (and highly traditional) learning system is that the self is not separate from the ideas and assumptions that form it. Kofman and Senge maintain that "our mental models are not like pieces of clothing that we can put on or take off. They are basic constitutive structures of our personality. For all intents and purposes, most of the time, we are our mental models."[3]

Community must be created in order for a classroom to both be managed and thrive. In her Tribes curriculum, Jeanne Gibbs (1978) sets forth a model of classroom interaction based upon community building. In this type of model, students:

- Actively participate
- Communicate and work well with others
- Value diverse abilities and cultural differences
- Assume responsibility for their own behavior
- Develop critical thinking and collaborative skills
- Improve their sense of self-worth and mastery of academics[4]

It is little coincidence that virtually all spiritual disciplines, regardless of culture or religious setting, are practiced in communities. Only with the support, insight, and fellowship of a community can we face the dangers of learning meaningful things.[5]

WHAT FISTICUFFS!

Competition is the second tentacle of the educational mon-
ster that thwarts real learning. Looking good becomes more
important than being good. The fear of not achieving at a
prescribed rate, in a prescribed fashion, is a nemesis of
learning and a catalyst for fear. In *No Contest: The Case Against
Competition,* author Alfie Kohn (1992) defines competition as
"mutually exclusive goal attainment." In order to have success, there must be failure. In order to gain, there must be
loss. Kohn's philosophy supports that of Kofman and Senge
(1995), who believe that in the United States, we tend to see
competition among individuals as the ultimate mechanism
for change and improvement in human affairs. However, the
reality is that competition is stressful: the possibility of failure
creates worry and agitation, thus hindering performance.

Competition, too, is cross-cultural. In an article on
parenting for *The Hindu,* Kalyanalakshmy Bhanumurthy
(1999) relates, "The general belief is that competition is the
only tool to make children achieve success in education and
in career. This view is so widely held that questioning it is
considered unrealistic, eccentric or even deviant." Bhanumurthy goes on to ask a critical question,

> The child's world of language and conceptual awareness
> thus expands, through comparison and contrast. Cogni-
> tive development proceeds apace. The comparison of
> material objects and phenomena gets extended to the
> comparison of human beings, violating without warning
> the sense of uniqueness and individuality. And when
> comparison becomes an emotional whiplash in the
> hands of a powerful adult, the child's world crumbles.
> Can such adults be considered civilised?[6]

Competition also reinforces the power of attaining only
short-term results. In *None of Our Business,* I note that it used
to be that the eternal question was "Which came first, the
chicken or the egg?" Our modern results-driven society has

46

formed a new answer to this query. It seems the reply en masse is a chorus of "Who cares, as long as we have an egg?" Today's students take less time to ponder, less time to process, and they move more quickly to producing outcomes than ever before. Author Susan Ohanian (2003) speaks of "speeding up the three-minute egg." Students are raised with the belief that faster must be better. And with the belief that better is important.

The implications of a competitive classroom environment for children who struggle in school are vast. First, consider that for every "winner," there must be twenty-five or more "losers." If a child is never on the receiving end of positive notes, stars on the wall, A's on a paper, praise from a teacher, or art pictures hung with pride, he begins to feel stress in his classroom.

I am sure that there are teachers who will read that last line and snort derisively, "Stress? You're telling me that Johnny feels stress? No way, Johnny *causes* stress." While the latter may be true, it is only because at some point in his school career, Johnny has undergone the demoralizing process of trying unsuccessfully to "do school" in the traditional way.

When I teach character education to groups of adults, they invariably applaud when I quote Michael Josephson's "Beware of the toxic effects of self-esteemia"[7] (2001). Self-esteemia concerns itself more with feeling good than being good. Thomas Lickona, an expert on the development of character, says that true character is "knowing the good, loving the good, and doing the good" (1992).[8] Both self-esteemia and Lickona's admonition are extremely important in the classroom management of students who struggle in school.

First, years of comparing themselves to classmates who are seemingly brighter, more artistic, more athletic, and more capable does cause dramatic issues of self-esteem for students, so much so that those students become at-risk within their educational environments. It is not that these students wish to feel good rather than being good; they simply see little value in engaging in teacher-pleasing behaviors when historically teachers have never been pleased. Often, there is little recognition, positive or negative, of school behaviors in their homes. And acting out or shutting down gives a student a role to play within a classroom. Students are accurate perceivers of roles, particularly because we teach them from childhood on to segregate. They say things like "That's Jeremy. He's really smart." Or "Julio is funny but he makes the teacher mad all the time." Or "Chandra never does her work. She just sits there and stares out the window." Note the qualifiers—*really, all the time, never*—which are markedly role-defining words.

The development of self-esteem should not be confused with the toxic effect of self-esteemia. Roger and David Johnson (1994), researchers in the field of cooperative learning, developed a list of common indicators of low self-esteem. Students who have low self-esteem:

1. Have low productivity due to setting low goals for themselves, lacking confidence in their ability, and assuming that they will fail no matter how hard they try.

2. Are critical of others as well as themselves by looking for flaws in others and trying to "tear them down."

3. Withdraw socially due to feeling awkward, self-conscious, and vulnerable to rejection.

4. Are conforming, agreeable, highly persuadable, and highly influenced by criticism.

5. Develop psychological problems such as anxiety, nervousness, insomnia, depression, and psychosomatic symptoms.[9]

The Johnsons further state that within competitive situations, self-esteem tends to be based on the contingent view of one's competence; for example, "If I win, then I have worth as a person, but if I lose, then I have no worth." Winners attribute their success to superior ability and attribute the failure of others to lack of ability, both of which contribute to self-aggrandizement. Losers, who are the vast majority, defensively tend to be self-disparaging and apprehensive about evaluation, and they tend to withdraw psychologically and physically. Within cooperative situations, individuals tend to interact, promote each other's success, form multidimensional and realistic impressions of each other's competencies, and give accurate feedback. Such interaction tends to promote a basic acceptance of oneself as a competent person.[10]

I believe that the toxic effect of self-esteemia has been caused by good intentions. Many teachers seek to recognize all students. They develop awards and send notes home and praise students whenever they are able. Both students and teachers, however, are acutely aware that an award for "most improved" is not the same as an award for "star pupil." Often, too, teachers struggle to match an award for a child, especially a behaviorally disruptive child. This causes them to feel resentful of having to try to come up with a compliment for the child who is the bane of their existence. The praise feels staged and false. Self-esteem has become secondary to the wish that Lance would stay in his chair, just once, for all of social studies class. Self-esteemia is born of the resentment of being nongenuine. The teacher doesn't feel like praising and subsequently the child does not feel praised. Eventually, this unhealthy pattern causes students to feel mistrustful of adult intentions and adults to feel like actors and not like teachers.

What then, is the remedy for that unlikable child in the fourth desk in the fifth row? Is it better to stay silent than to offer created praise? Yes, but silence alone is not a cure. The answer is a concentrated effort on behalf of the teacher to get to know the child, not just the child's behavior or grades. How does that child spend her weekends and her after-school hours? Does she excel in any of her art, music, or physical education classes? What did her teacher last year like about her? It sometimes takes the investigative techniques of

Sherlock Holmes to unravel the mystery of a struggling learner but professionalism requires that a teacher do exactly that. In the short run, it is easier to give created praise. In the long run, however, replacing self-esteemia with self-confidence is critical to the future of all children.

This leads to the second point of character development—knowing the good, loving the good, doing the good. As already mentioned in Chapter 1, it cannot be assumed that simply because a child has crossed the educational equator that he has the social or behavioral skills necessary for success. The first step for a teacher, then, is to make certain that his students know the behaviors that are expected in a classroom. It isn't enough to say "Respect others"; students and teachers alike must then brainstorm what respect looks like and sounds like. Everyone in the classroom must have a common definition of the qualities necessary to maximize learning.

Loving the good is a much more esoteric concept than the simple posting of a bevy of expectations. Perhaps an appropriate analogy is dieting. Most of us have learned enough about nutrition to know that a salad is healthier for us than a slice of pizza. We know that strawberries are more nutritious for a sweet tooth than chocolate. Yet we dip the strawberries in the chocolate and eat them with the pizza. Why? Because knowing the good is not enough. Loving the good, embracing it both intellectually and emotionally, is required before we can make a change and "do the diet." There are any number of factors that can finally cause an individual to "embrace the good." In the case of nutrition, perhaps a serious health condition, a burst of personal esteem, or a desire to fit into a new pair of jeans causes the transition from knowledge to practice. In the case of classroom management, it is most often the "relationship" mentioned in Chapter 2 that serves as the bridge between rules and evidence of positive behavior in a classroom. How, simply, does a teacher develop relationships? In the same way that a teacher learns to offer genuine praise—by getting to know each child in her classroom individually.

Replacing a traditional, competitive atmosphere with cooperation and character development is critical in a classroom for students who struggle. Cooperative learning requires positive interdependence, individual and group accountability, interpersonal skills, and the development of a community of caring within a classroom. Researchers Roger and David Johnson (1994) offer that positive interdependence results in promotive interaction. Promotive interaction is defined as individuals encouraging and facilitating each other's efforts to achieve, complete tasks, and produce in order to reach the group's goals. It is characterized by individuals providing each other with efficient and effective help and assistance.[11]

The adage about students not caring about how much a teacher knows until they understand how much that teacher cares has practical application in classroom management. Caring within a classroom can be taught as part of character education; yet it is larger than character education, too. Caring is a state of being within a classroom, transferred not only from a teacher to her students but from student to student as well. According to the Johnsons, "The more students care about each other, the harder they will work to achieve mutual learning goals. Long term and persistent efforts to achieve do not come from the head; they come from the heart."[12]

As mentioned in Chapter 2, there is often an intangible quality in working with students who struggle in school. It can perhaps be called an egocentrism. These students may have a muted ability to appreciate the perspectives of teachers and peers; they seem more driven by their individual wants and needs. It is difficult to determine the root of this quality—perhaps it is years of intellectual isolation in school, a home environment that provides minimal social interaction, or a manifestation of a factor of language development that is missing. Cooperative learning and character building help to bridge egocentric behavior and more socially conscious behavior. This process of teaching children respect for divergent viewpoints is often called social perspective taking. 'Alim Beveridge (2002) states,

> The development of perspective taking and empathy is important for moral growth because these two capabilities underlie the ability to interact with others justly and harmoniously. Because they are similar, these two capabilities are often confused, when, in fact, they are quite different. Perspective taking is a cognitive ability; it consists of being able to see the world from another's perspective. Empathy can be defined as "vicariously induced emotional reactions"; this definition, however, belies the fact that the word refers to a range of social, affective and attitudinal capabilities.[13]

Empathy skills are a natural component of a character-focused classroom. There are many canned character education programs available. Most offer a variety of materials and lesson plans suitable for a wide variety of grade levels. A benefit of such programs is that they are preplanned and offer a variety of activities. A drawback is that it's often difficult to find an additional twenty minutes of instructional time to teach a character-based skill.

I don't choose to use a canned character education program. Driven by a personal philosophy that true character education is infused into all the workings of a classroom, I prefer to develop a common language regarding the traits of character. I base my classroom practices on a model of character education called Character Counts!, as developed by the Josephson Institute of Ethics. The curriculum for the program is developed around six character traits: trust, respect, responsibility, fairness, caring, and citizenship.[14] There are lesson plans and activities available and sometimes I use them. More often, however, I use the academic lessons that the students encounter on a daily basis to connect to the common language of character that we've developed. It is impossible to discuss historical events without reflecting on the character traits of our heroes. Respect is a major part of any experiment conducted in a science class. Language arts is filled with stories of compassion, bravery, and courage. In the Character Counts! Program, each character trait is associated with a color in order to make it more memorable. Respect, for example, is yellow to trigger an association with the Golden Rule. I have all of the traits written in their corresponding color on the white board in my classroom. One day we had a visitor who asked the students the significance of the words on the board. Without hesitation, one of my students answered, "Those are our classroom rules" and the other students nodded in affirmation. I had never thought about it like that and had never introduced the traits in that manner. The students, however, felt themselves guided by the underlying principles that should guide us all. J. D. Rockefeller is quoted as saying, "I will pay more for the ability to deal with people than any other ability under the sun." He'd have been proud of the allegedly at-risk learners in my classroom.

A CHAIN GANG REACTION

Reactiveness is the third roadblock to natural learning. For most of us, reactiveness was reinforced on a daily basis in school. We solved problems identified by others, read what was assigned, wrote what was required. Gradually reactiveness became a way of life. Fitting in, being accepted, became more important than being ourselves. We learned that the way to succeed was to focus on the teachers' questions as opposed to our own. It is said that you can tell a great deal about a man by how he handles lost luggage, tangled Christmas tree lights, and rainy days. Reactiveness is a response conditioned by experience, modeling, and perception.

Students who struggle in school become victims of their experience. For reasons already discussed, they abandon a positive perception for a demoralized mentality. They often fail to see the healthy role models that are in their presence.

FAVORITE CHARACTER EDUCATION STORIES FOR DISCUSSION AND ACTIVITIES

The IALAC Story[15]

This IALAC story can be found at <http://www.os-iti.org/os/Snowflake.pdf>. I typically make up my own, suited for the age range of my audience. Before telling the story, each member of the group makes an IALAC sign. IALAC, which stands for "I Am Likable and Capable," is printed in the middle of the paper. The group member lists three things that make him likable and three things that he is good at. In addition, the student may put a symbol of himself on the page. As I tell the story and unpleasant things happen, I rip a piece of an IALAC sign that I have constructed for the story's lead character. Then I retell the story, creating positives instead of negatives, taping the IALAC sign back together. At the end, the group processes the activity, citing events from their own lives that have torn or recreated their personal IALAC signs. The group also discusses each person's influence over the invisible IALAC sign of another.

Sample story: Think of the boy who gets up in the morning with a big IALAC sign showing right straight across his chest. The first voice he hears is his father's, "Get out of bed, lazybones, or you'll never amount to anything." He goes on, "Did you get your homework done last night? If you only planned your studies better, you might get grades as good as your sister."

The boy gets out of bed, looks for his homework, and finds it rumpled up on the floor. He looks for his shoes and can't find them. His mother calls for him to hurry. He has to put on some old, worn-out tennis shoes with no shoelaces. He hurries down to breakfast. "What's for breakfast, Mom?"

She says, "You don't have time for anything but cereal. You're going to miss the bus." He gulps down the cereal and runs down the street to the bus stop.

The boy joins the other children waiting for the bus. One of the boys comes up behind him and knocks the books out of his hands. His homework, already rumpled, now ends up in a mud puddle. Quickly he gathers up his papers and books, gets on the bus, and sits all alone, as the other children have all found someone else to sit with.

In school, the teacher announces that there will be a spelling test. The boy feels okay about this because he did study spelling the night before, but he can't find his pencil—it must have dropped at the bus stop! He turns to the girl next to him, "May I borrow one of your pencils?"

She turns to him and says, "Bring your own pencils to school. I'm not giving you mine."

Later on when the children line up for recess, the teacher says, "I like the way the girls are lining up." On the playground, two boys have been selected to choose up sides for a kickball game. The boy waits to be chosen, but when everyone else is on a team, one of the boys says, "You take him. He's no good. He can't kick very well, or catch either."

During lunch, the boy is carefully carrying his tray to the table, when he trips and the tray goes clanging to the floor. No one helps. Everyone laughs.

After school, when the boy gets home, he calls out, "Mom, how about some milk and cookies?" But Mom isn't home. He remembers she had an appointment. He goes in to watch his favorite program on TV and settles down to be comfortable, when his big brother comes in and changes the station.

At supper, when everyone is eating and talking about the events of the day, he tries to get in a word about what happened to him during the day, but it seems that what everyone else has to say is more important and no one will listen.

By the time he gets ready for bed, the only thing remaining of his IALAC sign is a tiny piece just about big enough to cover the juice stain on his pajamas. The next morning when he wakes up, his IALAC sign is smaller than it was the previous morning. Will it get torn away again?

Wise Woman's Stone—A Story for Discussion

A wise woman who was traveling in the mountains found a precious stone in a stream. The next day she met another traveler who was hungry, and the wise woman opened her bag to share her food. The hungry traveler saw the precious stone in the wise woman's bag, admired it, and asked the wise woman to give it to him. The wise woman did so without hesitation.

The traveler left, rejoicing in his good fortune. He knew the jewel was worth enough to give him security for the rest of his life.

But a few days later he came back, searching for the wise woman. When he found her, he returned the stone and said, "I have been thinking. I know how valuable this stone is, but I give it back to you in the hope that you can give me something much more precious. If you can, give me what you have within you that enabled you to give me the stone."

Good News—A Story for the Discussion of Values[16]

Roberto deVincenzo, the great Argentine golfer, once won a tournament with a large sum of money as the purse. A woman approached him, asking for money, saying her child was seriously ill, near death, and she could not pay the doctor's bill. Touched by her plight, deVincenzo gave her the money he'd just won in the tournament.

The next week, an official with the golf association told him: "I have news for you. That woman has no sick baby. She's not even married. She fleeced you, my friend."

"You mean, there is no baby who is dying?" said deVincenzo.

"That's right," said the official.

"That's the best news I've heard all week," he replied.

Thus, their reactiveness to both curriculum and socialization efforts is skewed. A forcible return to a standardized curriculum that is meaningless to many learners will only serve to further warp reactiveness. The sanctions imposed by the No One is Left Behind the Child Act and its subsequent high-stakes assessments will foster a corruption of reactiveness that reaches far beyond the doors of a school. A narrow curriculum that trades experiential learning for fragmented facts and competitive scores not only alienates learners, but also deprives them of fundamental thought processes. Marion Brady (2000) states,

> When teaching is seen primarily as telling by means of teacher talk or textbook reading, the mental processes available to students dwindle down to just one: recall. Students may not be able to put their fingers on the reason schoolwork often frustrates and bores them, but its lack of genuine intellectual challenge is surely a factor. Here, again, is why the study of immediate, firsthand experience—the mall, the school, the street—can be so engaging. Its inherent complexity demands the use of every known thought process, and the level of difficulty automatically adjusts to that which is most appropriate to the individual student.[17]

HURRY UP SLOWLY

Common sense and curriculum are the best cures for reactiveness. Common sense can mean many things, but in the classroom management scenario it is best demonstrated by developmentally appropriate responses to student behavior. The media is filled with unfortunate examples of hostile or oppressive administrative responses to naïve behaviors of students. There are tales of first graders expelled from school for bringing kitchen knives, kindergartners suspended for playing cops and robbers, and middle schoolers suspended for snorting Kool-Aid.[18] The stories that make the headlines are certainly detrimental to the respect that real public education deserves. These stories are reactiveness in the most negligent form because administrators failed to determine the story behind the story. Consider the saga of the young man who was suspended from school for violating the three-cut policy by missing his family living class. On investigating the situation, a caring teacher discovered the reason behind the boy's behavior. Whenever his mother, a crack cocaine addict, received her government check, she cashed it and bought cocaine within minutes. The boy started waiting outside for the mailman in all types of weather. He intercepted the check, took it to the issuing bank, and waited for the manager, who gave him cash in envelopes. He took one envelope to pay the rent, another for food, another for utilities until all the family's bills were paid. By the time he arrived at school, he had missed family living.[19]

Dramatic examples should and do provoke dramatic responses of outrage among caring educators. But what about the less dramatic and more insidious kinds of reactiveness that are practiced daily in our schools? Anytime we ask students to move beyond their developmental readiness, we position ourselves to be reactive. The most common reactiveness can be found in two phrases that I've often heard repeated in faculty lounges, "What will he do when he is on the job?" and "How will she make it in the real world?" I heard this saying just the other day, in fact. My son, who has Attention Deficit Hyperactivity Disorder (ADHD), is very forgetful. He struggles with organization and has little concept of time. A highly visual-spatial and musically intelligent child, he thrives on band and choir, readily professing the joy that he finds in both. However, he often forgets his band lessons. I received a note home about his lack of concern and I called the school. It wasn't a lack of concern, I assured his teacher, but a developmental milestone that he has not yet reached. Changing the lesson time didn't help. Writing it in his agenda didn't help. And when he set an alarm on his wristwatch to remind him to go to band, he often left the watch at home. I asked his band teacher why someone couldn't simply call him to the lessons while we continued to work on his issues with time and forgetfulness. I patiently explained that he loved band, wasn't actively avoiding it like many children who purposefully miss lessons, and felt genuinely sorry when he forgot. The teacher acknowledged all of those things to be true but then added, "But it wouldn't be fair because then I'd have to call everyone." Everyone? Or only those concerned, ADHD, forgetful, or in need? Then the teacher made it a point to ponder aloud, "With his forgetfulness, I wonder what he'll do when he gets a job."

My son is twelve years old. Getting an adult job is at least six years away. When you think about it, that is one-third of his total years on Earth. I didn't worry that he would go to kindergarten in diapers or take a pacifier with him to first grade. I accepted that he would make appropriate developmental progress with my guidance. Common sense tells us that there are no prescriptive guidelines for growing children. It ought to tell us that there is no definition of fair. Reactiveness is guided by intellect and proactiveness is guided by intellect paired with heart. Curwin and Mendler (1999) advocate being as "tough as necessary" with regard to student discipline. This means using only the punitive measures that are necessary to promote safety in schools instead of blanket discipline. Schools must also be willing to view each student as a unique being and must use this new view to be as compassionate as necessary.[20] A sense of responsibility toward the growth and development of others is a civic virtue that must be modeled for students. And it will even help them when they get out in the real world.

IT'S ALL IN THE DELIVERY

A curriculum that is geared to the learning styles of each student can effectively curtail a great deal of academic reactiveness as well as mediate behavioral concerns. Engaged students are simply less likely to misbehave. Psychologist

Howard Gardner (1995) identified the following distinct types of intelligence:

Logical-mathematical intelligence consists of the ability to detect patterns, reason deductively, and think logically. This intelligence is most often associated with scientific and mathematical thinking. Children with this type of intelligence are interested in patterns, categories, and relationships. They are drawn to arithmetic problems, strategy games, and experiments.

Linguistic intelligence involves having a mastery of language. This intelligence includes the ability to effectively manipulate language to express oneself rhetorically or poetically. It also allows one to use language as a means to remember information. Children with this kind of intelligence enjoy writing, reading, telling stories, or doing crossword puzzles.

Spatial intelligence gives one the ability to manipulate and create mental images in order to solve problems. This intelligence is not limited to visual domains—Gardner notes that spatial intelligence is also formed in blind children. These children think in images and pictures. They may be fascinated with mazes or jigsaw puzzles, or spend free time drawing, building with Legos, or daydreaming.

Musical intelligence encompasses the capability to recognize and compose musical pitches, tones, and rhythms. Musical children are always singing or drumming to themselves. They are usually quite aware of sounds others may miss. These kids are often discriminating listeners.

Bodily-kinesthetic intelligence is the ability to use one's mental abilities to coordinate one's own bodily movements. These kids process knowledge through bodily sensations. They are often athletic, dancers, or good at crafts such as sewing or woodworking.

Interpersonal intelligence involves the ability to understand and discern the feelings and intentions of others. Children who are leaders among their peers, who are good at communicating, and who seem to understand others' feelings and motives possess interpersonal intelligence.

Intrapersonal intelligence reflects the ability to understand one's own feelings and motivations. These children may be shy. They are very aware of their own feelings and are self-motivated.

In later works, Gardner identified an eighth type of intelligence. **Naturalist intelligence** allows people to distinguish among, classify, and use features of the environment. Farmers, gardeners, botanists, geologists, florists, and archaeologists all exhibit this intelligence, as do students who can name and describe the features of every make of car around them.[21]

A parent recently shared with me that her second grader came home from school after a field trip claiming, "We didn't learn anything today." Yet her daughter was filled with new information and ideas. Her learning had been so natural and engaging that it didn't seem like the focused effort that had become the norm. I remember that when I was in third grade, I learned the times tables through a series of cassettes that set the math facts to music. Amazingly, I still remember some of those songs even now, thirty years later. When we got to the study of conjunctions in my language class, I was surprised to hear a few of my students immediately begin singing the Schoolhouse Rock song, "Conjunction Junction." A teacher of gifted and talented children shared the story of a visual-spatial learner who did not want to give any of his toys to charity. His mother was puzzled because her son was normally a very giving person. Upon questioning his motives, she learned that he didn't want to give away his toys because "Then I am giving away my memories." The sight of his toys literally transported him back in time to the happy memories that he had developed while playing with them. I witnessed the revelation of reading come to a first grader when it was finally made kinesthetic to him. He stretched his arms toward the ceiling on the first consonant in the word *cat*. He touched his pudgy belly on the vowel and he reached for his toes on the "t." He evidenced his new skill in a series of calisthenics that were an inspiring tribute to the multiple intelligences in action. The theory of multiple intelligences is one of the chief practices of an academically responsive classroom. Gardner writes,

> Without a doubt, one of the reasons that MI theory has attracted attention in the educational community is because of its ringing endorsement of an ensemble of propositions: we are not all the same, we do not all have the same kinds of minds; education works more effectively for most individuals if these differences in mentation and strengths are taken into account rather than denied or ignored. I have always believed that the heart of the MI perspective—in theory and in practice— inheres in taking human differences seriously. At the theoretical level, one acknowledges that all individuals cannot be profitably arrayed on a single intellectual dimension. At the practical level, one acknowledges that any uniform educational approach is likely to serve only a minority of children.[22]

WHAT GOES AROUND . . .

Experienced educators often learn to close their classroom doors and do what works best for the children in their charge. They often turn a deaf ear to theory or to innovation, recognizing each as a part of the educational wheel that has gone around many times before. They do not want to be behaviorists, traditionalists, standardistos, or constructivists. They simply want to be teachers.

History, however, has a way of repeating itself and without ongoing professional development, there will be few improvements to the educational wheel. The first blending of best practice combines behaviorism and individualized learning. World-famous behaviorist B. F. Skinner, after noting that all students in his daughter's classroom were expected to progress at prescribed rates, even when they were unable to do so, designed the model of a teaching machine.

> For Skinner, the beauty of the machine was that he had designed it so that the pace at which the lesson proceeded was determined by the individual student; thus, students could progress as quickly or as slowly as they desired or needed. For a brief historical moment, then, the concept of teaching machines and their preliminary attempt to tend to at least some basic needs of the individual enjoyed immense popularity. Indeed, Sidney Pressey, another developer of teaching machines, described this hopeful vision of education: "Work in the schools of the future will be marvelously though simply organized, so as to adjust almost automatically to individual differences and to the characteristics of the learning process."[23]

A focus on the individual, however, was proven not to be adequate in addressing the vast educational needs of students. The theory of constructivism came into being. Constructivism is often discussed in a social context. That is, the construction of knowledge is influenced by people's interactions with other people. In addition, some theorists assert that people and their approaches to learning and knowledge construction are influenced by the norms and practices of the communities and culture in which they matured. Culture involves not only an external environment, but also the human activity within that environment. Socioculturalism, as the theory dealing with these issues is known, subsequently argues that the kinds of knowledge an individual can learn to use and the ways in which she learns them are constrained by the culture in which she matured.[24]

The best answer to reactiveness is proactiveness. Proactiveness can be achieved by the fostering of academic responsiveness within a classroom. Academic responsiveness is the new blend of educational theory—individualized constructivism. Both constructivism and responsiveness will be discussed in greater detail in Chapter 5. Students should be allowed to participate in decisions about their education. Learning becomes a habit of mind if natural curiosities are sated at reasonable developmental paces. Additionally, students are educated as part of a greater societal whole. They are contributors not only to their own learning, but they are also responsible for the system of learners surrounding them. Henry B. Adams is known for saying that "a teacher affects eternity; he can never tell where his influence stops." We are all teachers and we are all learners, from the tiniest voice in the back of a first-grade classroom to the commanding edicts of a central government. Let's use our power wisely.

CHAPTER FOUR

CREATING COHESIVENESS

How to Be an Energizer Educator and Reach
All *Students in Your Classroom*

NEWTON'S FIRST LAW

Students in motion tend to stay in motion . . . or so it seems. There has been a dramatic increase in the diagnosis of Attention Deficit Hyperactivity Disorder (ADHD) in our country in recent years. According to "A.D.D.—A Dubious Diagnosis?", an investigative report on Ritalin and ADD produced by the Merrow Report and aired on PBS in 1995, an estimated two million children in America are currently receiving medication as treatment for ADD or ADHD. As an eighth grader at a school in Maryland, Matt Scherbel wrote a diatribe about the negative effects of Ritalin. He wrote about how the drug made him feel unlike himself for six hours a day. His answer to the medication question lay in his expectation of his education: "The schools should shape our education around our idiosyncratic minds, our quaint minds, our quirky minds, our crackpot minds, our curious minds. Where would we be without eccentric people?"[1]

The ongoing debate about overdiagnosis, underdiagnosis, or whether "those kids just ought to learn to behave" is a moot point for many teachers. Theory must grapple with sociology outside of the classroom doors because in spite of the struggle, the seat next to the teacher's desk is always occupied. There is a palpable energy that runs through ADHD kids. It is more than their unraised hands, their incessant chatter, and the frequent sharpening of their pencils. It is greater than the drumming on the desk, the shuffling feet, and the thrice-an-hour requests to go and get a drink. It is a life force that permeates outward from them. Sometimes that force is so great that the cart overtakes the horse. It's the childhood feeling of running down a hill . . . both exhilarating in its freedom and frightening in the secret fear that our feet may not stop.

Yet, as the title of this book suggests, we do not often let children run downhill. Instead, we command them upward. School is a difficult place for children whose feet were meant to fly.

ALPHABET SOUP

I've always taught the "alphabet kids"—that is, those students who have the scarlet letters of a disability on their cumulative folders. Even now, in working with students who don't have special education labels, there is still the invisible brand of "at-risk." I've never quite understood the professional purpose of labeling. I realize, of course, that there is a practical purpose. Students are categorically labeled in order to receive federal funds. They are grouped according to a predefined set of traits in order to receive appropriate services. I liken this to the fact that my house has a number. The number means that I will receive my mail. My driver's license has a number, too, and a special label about wearing corrective lenses. I understand the necessity of that, too. Yet, as important as both those labels are, none of my colleagues address me as "1811." None of my friends call me "Organ Donor." No salesman has ever clapped me on the shoulder and boomed, "Welcome, Corrective Lens Wearer." It's absurd to think that in our personal and professional worlds, we are considered labels. We are, instead, people with unique gifts, talents, and quirks. Why then, do so many good-hearted and well-intentioned educators allow a label to make them into an educational Cyclops? A myopic view of any student, but especially a special education student, places that student at risk. Not only is it an uphill journey, but that student must also hold the steaming bowl of alphabet soup, careful not to spill it as she travels on her way. Such treatment is unfair. It's unkind and it's educationally hazardous. Take it from me, number 1811.

THAT SMARTS!

"Will you draw for me, Alvaro?" could often be heard in my classroom during Alvaro's seventh- and eighth-grade years. Alvaro is a gifted artist and the other students recognized his natural talent. He was flattered by their requests and almost always obliging. He enjoyed being able to do what he loved and to be admired for it. School was otherwise difficult for him and his artistic talent allowed him to shine. Yet sometimes, there was frustration in his smile and hesitancy in his hand. He often had to interrupt his own projects to assist. Sometimes, it seems, he became tired of his talent. Sometimes, too, the others were resentful. They were jealous that they could not produce the consistent level of quality that Alvaro was able to bring to his art.

"Yer, would you mind reading with Christine? Could you take just a minute and help Brandon? Do you have time to do flashcards with Dillon?" The academically gifted are a great classroom resource. Teachers rely on their consistency and their abilities. It is comforting to know that our educational message is being delivered and our gifted students often give clear feedback on our delivery. They are able to demonstrate learning in a variety of ways. Yet sometimes, they get tired. Sometimes they get bored. And often they are resented by their classmates. Flattery gives way to annoyance as their teachers hold up their projects and say, "Class, this is what an A project looks like." They shrink in their seats as the class rolls its eyes and sighs. On the next project, they decide to dummy it down a bit. It is a vicious cycle.

Giftedness. Special Education. Attention Deficit Hyperactivity Disorder (ADHD). All these words are synonymous with opportunity—and all are invitations for risk. It is not, however, a deductive process. It is not true that all gifted, special education, or ADHD children are at-risk. It is not even true that the current educational environment poses a risk to all such learners. However, the traits expressed by all three groups compound the threat of risk. Add to these factors the contentious relationships at the onset of adolescence and we have the perfect formula for frustration, alienation, school failure, and school dropout.[2]

FRONT LINES AND FAULT LINES

The first remedy towards creating whole learners out of all learners is to stop engaging in educational probate. It is time to call a moratorium on blame, diagnosis, and debate and to simply start dealing with the students who are seated in the desks or at the tables in our classrooms. Specific education for the gifted and talented has struggled since its inception. It is federally recommended and not federally required. This means that districts often do the minimum level of service required to appease vocal parents and to compete with neighboring districts. There are many school administrators, teachers, and members of the public who refuse to acknowledge that those with an academic gift or an outstanding talent don't simply have an easy road. They do not understand that intelligence without appropriate affect is as damaging to students as affect without accompanying intellect. Even when faced with the statistics of a bell-shaped curve, they understand the necessity of providing alternative services for a child whose IQ is 70 but do not comprehend the need for services for a child whose IQ is 130. The 30 standard deviation points that qualify the learner have more power in a downward direction.

Overdiagnosed? Overmedicated? Underfunded? Misunderstood? Undisciplined? Students with ADHD may be any of these or they may be none of them. ADHD is a medical condition determined by a doctor. Clearly, there are cases of misdiagnosis. Sometimes, parents without skills raise children with impulsive, disorganized, and hyperactive behaviors. While these children may not be classically ADHD, they certainly evidence ADHD behaviors. I will never forget second-grader Joshua. He was the first child to open my eyes to the impact of ADHD as a medical condition. Joshua screamed his way through first grade. He hit his peers, yelled obscenities at everyone, and seemed to enjoy digging his pearly white teeth into tender teacher flesh whenever possible. As a second-year teacher, I was cowed by the knowledge that I needed to get a tetanus shot for a human bite. Joshua never stopped moving and was incapable of sitting at a desk. He knew all of his letters, all of the sounds, and could read very well. He couldn't draw or write and he sacrificed many a pencil in his rage at being unable to do so.

Joshua's seven-year-old world rapidly deteriorated both at home and at school. He was becoming too much for his well-intentioned single mother to handle. His little brother was cooperative and quiet and Joshua's mother didn't understand her first-born feral child. She took him to a doctor who immediately began treating him for ADHD. On his first day with medication, Joshua sat at his desk. He raised his hand. He could print legibly. He didn't bite anyone all day.

Does that mean that medication is the answer? No, it means that medication was the answer for Joshua. There have been countless other students diagnosed with ADHD who have needed dietary changes, behavioral remediation, consistency in parenting, or a combination of all of these. What matters is that the condition and the child are not ours to judge—they are ours to educate.

The National At-Risk Educator's Network (NAREN) uses a bumblebee as a symbol of the organization. The reason for doing so is profound.

> Because of its unwieldy body and disproportionately small wing size, scientists studying aerodynamics once stated that, technically, the bumblebee should be incapable of flying. And yet fly it does. Many people—including far too many educators, counselors and social workers—believe that trying to educate and train at-risk kids is a waste of time because they will never amount to much anyway. Many of these kids do still learn to fly despite the great weights they often carry inside them. Fly, many most certainly can and do; and fly, they all most certainly could, with better informed and more supportive educational stakeholders.[3]

Special education students are at risk of becoming bumblebees, too. It is an atrocity when teachers seek to make their own lives easier by denying special education students access to a field trip because they are educated out of the mainstream. I have worked with children written off because of their educational label and I have worked with teachers who seemed to desire a label for every student in their classroom. I have also worked with countless caring, giving, welcoming teachers who bent over backwards to view all students in their charge as unique learners. I've always felt that it was a positive that such teachers are internally rewarded for their displays of open-mindedness. The explicit educational response is to simply shift more needy learners into their classrooms. Unfair? Inequitable? Maybe, but that doesn't matter to the learning disabled (LD) student with his hand waving in the air.

Theoretically, the ongoing debates about what is educationally sound are not only appropriate, they are necessary to promote change. Practically, however, they do not help a teacher to meet the just-in-time (JIT) needs of her students. Judgments and debates become immoral when they influence inaction in a classroom. When a teacher waits for ser-

70

vices, passes the educational buck to a specialist, decreases expectations due to a label, or fails to create an individually constructivist curriculum, she is engaging in a process of educational probate that diminishes the will of the child.

THE ENERGIZER EDUCATOR

In a comprehensive tome dedicated to the unique needs of visual-spatial learners, Linda Kreger Silverman (2002) offers several keys for success for "twice exceptional" learners. Several pieces of her advice extend to at-risk learners with any of the multiple intelligences.

1. Show them, don't just tell them. Teach them to picture concepts.
2. Use hands-on learning experiences.
3. Don't make them show their work—let them find the answers their own way.
4. Avoid timed tests.
5. Allow the use of a computer for all written work.
6. Give them advanced concepts even if they haven't mastered easier work.
7. Expose them to role models of successful twice exceptional individuals.
8. Let them tape-record lectures.
9. Use earphones to block out auditory distractions.
10. Have a place in the classroom where they can retreat when they are overstimulated.
11. Shorten written assignments and allow them to be dictated.
12. Allow the use of a calculator.[4]

I called this section the energizer educator because a good educator keeps going and going. He keeps searching for the teaching techniques that will best match the learning styles of his students. The energizer educator recognizes his profession as an immersion into lifelong learning. This teacher extends himself beyond the hours of the school day. He marches past the critics who tell him that giving tests orally is enabling or that modifying expectations is unfair. Energizer educators have self-confidence; an ongoing commitment to creativity, flexibility, and quality; and an ability to trust students. In addition to these traits, an exemplary teacher must have the ability to keep up with the children's high energy levels and constant questioning. The teacher must have an almost limitless ability to listen and must have the stamina to direct, redirect, and respond appropriately, seemingly ad infinitum. Finally, the teacher must possess a tolerance for students with high levels of curiosity, for independent and creative thought, and for frequent challenges to the existing way of doing things.[5]

"Humor isn't for everyone . . . just those who want to have fun, enjoy life, and feel alive." This quote by Anne Wilson Schaef highlights another essential quality of the energizer educator. Dr. Stuart Robertshaw, also known as Dr. Humor, is known nationally for his motivational efforts to encourage everyone to infuse more humor into their lives. In 1987 a publisher asked him to review a textbook on child development. "There was a chapter on joy, creativity and humor in young children," Robertshaw recalls, "and there was a quote that got my attention. It said that, on the average, preschool children laugh or smile 400 times a day, but adults over the age of 35 laugh or smile only 15 times a day."

That set Robertshaw to researching the subject. He'd always been a humor collector, keeping files of cartoons and funny stories. But he started looking deeper. "I spent about four hours a week for the next three months in the library reading about humor," he says. He was amazed at what he found—for instance, medical studies showing that laughter lowered blood pressure and produced endorphins, the body's natural painkillers.[6]

Much of the resistance to using humor in the adult world comes from the seriousness of our schooling. Why bother using humor when you can make a point as fiercely as possible and get on with it? Author Marshall McLuhan has an answer: "Those who draw the distinction between education and entertainment don't know the first thing about either." Think about it. When we're babies, we're trained to expect good things of people. We encourage playfulness even into the first few years of school. Then the same behavior that your teachers rewarded you for in the earlier years of school got you sent to the principal's office by the fifth and sixth grade.[7]

A basic tenet of building relationships is to "do no harm." This maxim is critical to the use of humor in a classroom. Any humor that uses stereotypes or put-downs, or that encourages a negative atmosphere does harm. Positive humor, however, serves to unify and relax students, creating ideal conditions for learning.

My seventh-grade math class was really struggling with algebraic equations. I was at the board using different-colored markers and attempting to show the difference between a "5y" and a "5." I drew a dog's head around the first number and a cat's head around the second. I told the students that trying to add the two was like trying to mix cats with dogs. Later in the lesson, I asked a student who was struggling, "Can you mix cats and dogs together?" His response was "Sure, but you get a mutant." The entire class burst into laughter and the tone of "no mutants in math class" was set. The group was cohesive, motivated, and their collective sense of frustration with the mathematical concept was greatly reduced.

In my first year as a teacher, I had a long, narrow special education classroom. In the name of student management, I segregated it, putting up walls and dividers to separate the most disruptive of my learners. Fresh from the university and armed with the belief that I was responsible for the complete control of student actions, I behaved like a drill sergeant for much of the day, allocating points for positive behaviors and redirecting negative behaviors time and time again. Yet my classroom was most functional when my students all sat at the common table and learned together.

Slowly the walls came down and my students began to feel a sense of group accountability.

It is my firm belief that classrooms must be fluid, tolerant, and cohesive. The expectation of positive character traits, the infusion of humor, and an atmosphere of accountability create a familial bond among learners. This connection is integral to students who are at-risk. Unification implies shared power. When a student started to decorate his "cubicle" in that first year of teaching, I came to the startling realization that I was actually giving him and the others who were "walled off" more power. This was especially highlighted by the fact that his décor of choice was Playboy centerfolds!

Fourteen years after that first year, in a new school district, equipped with a classroom the size of a shoebox and ten animated "at-risk" seventh graders before me, I made a simple announcement. "This is our space. We are all responsible for it. We are all responsible for each other. We don't have to even like one another to respect one another but it sure would help. So try to find one likable thing about everyone in here." That class was together for two years and moved into a larger room during the second year. The students commented on occasion that they missed the "forced togetherness" of the previous classroom. During the first year, the class of ten expanded into twelve; they grew taller, broader, and more tolerant. They went through all the stages of group development—they formed, they normed, they stormed, and they performed. And many of them cried when it was time to say goodbye and move on to the high school because they felt as if they were disbanding a family.

15 MPH IN SCHOOL ZONES

Many facets of the educational environment are controlled for both students and staff. We are told what to teach, when to teach it, when to use the restroom, when to eat lunch, and when to head for home. Often this guidance comes in the form of a master schedule enforced by a series of bells.

Teachers are great companions on long-distance car trips because we've learned to forestall our biological urges for forty-seven minutes or more of instructional time. The mechanisms that regulate the school day are put into place for a variety of reasons; safety, convenience, and curriculum all affect the boundaries of a student's day.

Just as there are components that protect the functions of an institution, so, too, the inner workings of a classroom and the individual methodology of an instructor create miniature learning zones within that institution. "Educator, know thyself" is perhaps the best advice that can be given— maximal learning is dependent upon fluidity, tolerance, and cohesion and those intangible traits are directly reflected in a teacher's style.

Whether defining a curriculum, resolving a conflict, or infusing humor into instruction, a teacher performs best when he is true to his own personal style. I used to love to go into the classroom of a colleague, Bob, and watch him teach. His classroom was always decorated cheerfully and tastefully. Personal photographs adorned his desk, plants grew in all corners of the room, and there were several pieces of artwork that reflected his own whimsical nature. He always greeted each of the students warmly and by name. He inquired after family members who had been his students in years gone past. He had nicknames for the students who needed extra attention and it was obvious that everyone present felt comfortable and safe. He began each of his social studies classes by allowing the students to read the daily newspaper and discuss the headlines. It was a practice that only took five minutes but it allowed all voices and opinions to be heard. Students could comment on any article, ranging from the national news to a local editorial to the latest antics of Charlie Brown, or students could simply read the paper without commenting at all.

Bob was also a master at pacing his curriculum. The newspapers would rustle and I would shuffle in my seat, convinced, at first, that too much instructional time was passing by. I knew that Bob had a full agenda for each day and I never failed to be amazed by the natural grace that propelled him through his lesson plans. He would frequently stop to ask questions, tell personal anecdotes, or allow the students to share thoughts, and he still accomplished all that he set out to do.

As a middle school principal, I was able to watch many effective teachers in action. I witnessed language teachers bound by grammar texts and those who never opened the book. I saw hands-on science in well-equipped laboratories and science taught in sparse classrooms without even running water. I heard teachers insist on correct spellings and others who simply said "Do your best." I was immersed in classrooms alive with technology and in others where a notebook and a pencil were the most appropriate tools. Time and again I discovered that authentic individuals are the most effective teachers. Classroom practices vary widely but educators who are comfortable with themselves, believe in their methodologies, and have genuine positive feelings for students create environments that are ripe for real learning.

AND THESE THREE THINGS REMAIN

The only child of neatnik, structured parents, I am a self-professed "relaxed whirlwind" who always has to trudge down to the Department of Motor Vehicles and pay an extra fee to recover the title and registration for my car because I've inevitably misplaced the original. While being both laid-back and a whirlwind may seem an oxymoron, I can assure you both from personal experience and from extensive work with students who struggle in school that it is not. It is not only possible to have eight fingers in eight pies while seated in one chair—it is how many of us live our lives. It is the ability to first organize, then generalize, and finally to transition successive skills that allows individuals to wear a plethora of hats and successfully perform a variety of unrelated tasks.

When I was about eight, I discovered a terrific way to clean my room. I simply opened up my top dresser drawer, removed the clothing, swept the contents of a dresser top replete with soda cans, tissues, and apple cores into the drawer, and then shoved the clothing back on top. It even looked neat when my mother came to inspect. Of course, not everything fit into the drawers with the clothing, and thus the corners of the closets and the crevices of the toy box were also always overflowing with any number of treasures and a fair amount of refuse. This worked, of course, until my mother began to wonder why I never carried anything *out* of my bedroom and why my sweatshirts began to smell like a vintage apple orchard well after harvesting time. It was then that I learned that organization needs both a purpose and a plan.

Students must be taught both the purpose and the plan of organization. Purpose answers the question about why organization is important. Is it because an adult inspector will check their work? It is so that assignments can be found? Is it so that they can get to their classes on time and have the necessary materials? Is it so that they don't have to listen to the teacher badger them about the mess beneath their desk?

Purpose is important because it reflects motivation. In my early days of cleaning, I was motivated only by my mother's stamp of approval so that I could be finished with my chores and play outside. Later, after more than a few lost treasures prompted hours of searching and gallons of tears, I was motivated by a more internal desire to keep things that were precious to me. Still later in life, I was nudged toward increased orderliness in order to get to work on time, maintain a good credit rating, and have a presentable home.

Disenfranchised students often lack purpose because they lack both external and internal motivation. Before a teacher can even begin to help a student build a plan for organization, she must establish a sense of purpose. One of the best ways to do this is to make organization both rewarding and nonthreatening. A kind word and a pocketful of Starburst candies go a long way in providing a purpose for organization. When I first meet a group of students, I compliment them when they have their materials in class; sometimes, I provide an intermittent reinforcement in the form of a piece of candy to those students who are prepared. I write positive notes home, send them with a complimentary note to the principal, or allow them to leave a few minutes early at the end of the day or at lunchtime as an acknowledgement that organization is of value in my classroom. I also ask them probing questions about their motivation and the plans behind their organization. I make it a point to let the other students know that organization is not easy and that Jim or Nakama is not simply lucky. I ask questions such as, "How did you know what to bring to class today? Where did you keep it so that you could find it? Do you always keep things there? When did you start doing that? Did it take you a while to get organized like that? Are there any positives associated with your organizational system? Are there any negatives? Would you recommend it to other people?"

When students are not organized or prepared, I empathize. I let them know that I struggle with staying organized, too. I tell them that their lack of organization is a problem in my classroom and I ask them if they have a solution for solving it. If they don't, I remind them that we are a team of learners and offer to ask the class for suggestions. Some students welcome this and others quickly come up with at least one solution. My goal is not to outline a lifetime fraught with difficulty due to a chaotic personal style, but rather to instill an initial sense of purpose. I finish by asking my students what their solution is for "today" and then for "tomorrow." A "today" solution might mean borrowing the necessary materials from a friend, going to a locker (and staying after school), or using something from the "kid cupboard" in the classroom. A "tomorrow" solution might be writing in the assignment notebook, scribbling a note on an arm, or making a decision to keep materials in the classroom for a while. This is the beginning of a development of a plan.

Providing students an underlying purpose by using positive words, edible treats, or reinforcement from others doesn't always work. Students may feel manipulated or simply wish to be oppositional. Usually, I have a private conversation with those students. I acknowledge that using small rewards is a way to inspire organization. I agree that it is somewhat manipulative. And then I tell them that it is only because I care. I tell them that because I care, I try to make learning life skills somewhat painless and that organization is a life skill. I also tell students that they will always have my acceptance and that I will like them in spite of their behavior but that I will never permit them to be without purpose, either. In short, I tell them that I will keep bugging them because organization is important and that having a purpose and a plan are even more important. Eventually, most students smile and tell me that they'll get a purpose if only I'll stop talking. I smile back and ask them for a "tomorrow" plan.

When I speak of goal setting with students, I use the words "today" and "tomorrow" very specifically. Students who struggle in school typically do not have the capacity to think about long-term goals. The stresses of their immediate worlds take up too much of their care and their intellect and they cannot envision "ten years from now when you get a job." The term *staging* refers to dividing tasks into small units and performing each subtask independently; staging is a very effective way to encourage purposeful, planned organization for students. Thus, "I want you to have an organizational plan for language class tomorrow" has more validity to students than "I want you to have a plan for not misplacing any more work." Often, it has taken years for students to achieve the state of chaos that they are immersed in, and it is unrealistic to expect immediate and global progress. We are often in a professional hurry because we don't have the luxury of time. We want to give Greg all of the organizational proficiencies necessary in one large lesson because we fear for his academic future if he does not possess those skills. The truth of the matter is, though, that Greg does not possess the skills, must learn them as progressively as he has learned other life skills, and that time is not on our side. Just as we would not hand a primer to a nonreader and command them to read, we cannot expect Greg to generalize all of the skills he needs quickly and adeptly.

SPECIFIC PLANS FOR TEACHING ORGANIZATIONAL SKILLS

Two Folders

Most disorganized students are overwhelmed by the traditional "folder for every class" system. Instead, the student should simply use two folders, one for work to be finished and turned in and one for work that has been graded. It is important that the student be given time and adult supervision with the daily sorting of papers into the folders. The only task of sorting is to place papers into appropriate piles. It is not the time to discuss incomplete work. Once the work is sorted, the student should develop and share with an adult a plan for the contents of the "unfinished" folder.

Lockers and Desks

Disorganized students need a plan for cleaning out lockers and desks. It is overwhelming to them to hear "clean your desk." Often, they will remove only the noticeable trash and simply heap the rest of the contents into a more organized pile. Instead, an adult needs to break down the task. "I want you to put all the loose papers in a pile" could be a first step. When that step is completed, the next direction should be given, "Put all the things you write or color with in one pile." This process would continue until the contents of the desk were organized. On future "cleaning trips" a teacher might remind a class about how they cleaned their lockers last time and ask the students to write a list showing the sequence to be used in tidying their personal space.

Space Within a Classroom

When it is practical, it is extremely helpful to provide a small space within the classroom for a student's materials. Some teachers allow students to keep textbooks in the classroom so that they can be prepared for class. Others keep a store of materials for students to use. A personal space, however, also allows a student to keep items of importance inside a classroom and helps them to feel connected to the learning environment. I've discovered that my students will store items in "secret" places within the classroom if they don't have a cubby or a desk or a shelf to call their own.

Looks Like, Sounds Like, Feels Like

It is helpful to discuss with students, either as a group, or individually, what good organization looks like, sounds like, and feels like. A chart with three columns can be made to show the positive effects of organization. It is important to brainstorm ideas with students. Examples might be: Organization looks like having a pencil and a notebook, like writing in an agenda, or like putting all homework in the correct folder. Organization sounds like, "Here is my homework, Mrs. Smith" and like "I can find that in my locker." The feelings associated with organization may be *confident, less hassled by teachers,* or *satisfied.*

Positive Envisioning

In all situations with students, whether it is in the formation of basic organizational skills or in the later generalization or transition of those habits, positive envisioning allows them to get a picture of success in their minds. Students will feel strange, at first, creating a mental picture of themselves arriving on time to class with all of their materials. It is best to start with non-threatening envisioning, such as "Imagine yourself winning the lottery. What does your face look like? Which store in the mall would you visit first? Picture yourself walking through the mall. Feel the linoleum under your feet. You're at the store, what is the first thing that you touch there?" From exercises like this one, you can lead to more mature envisioning. For instance, "Imagine that you stayed up late last night and did your homework and

that you put it in your backpack. When you get to class,
picture yourself reaching into that backpack and pulling
out the homework. How does the teacher respond? How
do you feel?" Students can give a positive visualization
to most school situations and may feel more secure in
attempting to match their behaviors to the representation
in their heads.

THE MODERN MAJOR GENERALIZATION

After developing a purpose and a plan for organization, students must learn to generalize skills between subject areas first
within the classroom and then to transition those abilities
across all subject areas. The *Dimensions of Learning* model
(DOL) states that learning does not stop with acquiring and
integrating knowledge. Learners develop in-depth understanding through the process of extending and refining their
knowledge (e.g., by making new distinctions, clearing up mis-
conceptions, and reaching conclusions). They rigorously ana-
lyze what they have learned by applying reasoning processes
that will help them extend and refine the information.[8]

A crucial but often unrecognized dimension of learning
is the capacity to make use of prior experience as well as
emerging experience in new situations. It is necessary to
observe learners over a period of time while they engage in a
variety of activities in order to account for the development
of this important capability, which is at the heart of creative
thinking and its application.[9] Ongoing observation and
reflection are critical to successful generalization of behaviors. Students who struggle in school typically have difficulty
making consistent connections across environments, often
because there is a vast difference between their school,
home, and community. As a school principal, I sometimes
had students use my office phone to call a parent and tell
them about the conversation they had just had with me

regarding some misbehavior. My dialogue with the students was typically calm, probing, focused, and optimistic of future behavioral change. I remember talking with Jared one spring day about his frequent outbursts in class. Throughout our discussion he was respectful, sharing not only that sitting still was difficult for him but also that he was upset with a good friend. Because it was not Jared's first time in the office for similar behavior, he also received a consequence and the directive to call his mother and share our discussion and his consequence with her. Before Jared could even complete his story and his subsequent plan of action, I could hear his mother screaming and shouting curses at him over the phone. Certainly Jared had a purpose and a plan and an ability to generalize respectful behavior as far as my office door, but the struggle to maintain that behavior on a daily basis across environments was a burden for him. The positive modeling found in schools is only a small portion of the modeling present in a child's home and community. In Chapter 5, I'll address positive strategies for working with parents and community members to effect more fluid (and more likely) change for students. It is more than the village that raises a child; it is the quality, the character, and the caring of that village. A karate instructor who worked with my students for nine weeks had this to say on leadership, "If you want to know if you're a good leader, look behind you and watch what your followers are doing. If they are on the right track, so are you." It is vital that all who influence children know the good, do the good, and love the good. It is the only way to love the children.

CHAPTER FIVE

CREATING CONTINUITY

*Making Your Curriculum Flow, Encouraging Your
Students to Care, and Validating Your Successful
Alternative Programs*

DEAR JOHN

"The one memory that I would give away would be
school—like the hard work that has to be done on time
and the rushing of getting the work done on time—like
sitting in a chair and trying to finish a paragraph or
something that can't get finished . . . I don't enjoy school
but I have to go to school. That's the memory that I have
to give away."

One of my students wrote those words in response to an
assignment about a memory that they would give away if they
could. He is a quiet student, organized, polite, and of average ability. Yet school is the bane of his existence. He goes
every day to a job that he hates. It is for students like David
that the educational system needs to change. It is also for students like Tanya, who is loud, aggressive, and hostile. She
lets everyone know that school is her jailer. She performs
poorly when she performs at all. Programmatic changes are
necessary to address these two extremes and the thousands
of faces that fall in between them.

Data is getting better. Sociologists are better able to
track both the reasons and the ramifications of failing to

complete school. Most dropouts indicate that both their personal and school lives were very difficult prior to their departure from school. The statistics support that precedent. In a survey of eighteen-year-old dropouts,

- 20 percent were married, divorced, or living as married. Nearly 40 percent had or were expecting a child.
- Nearly 25 percent changed schools two or more times.
- 12 percent ran away from home.
- Almost 20 percent were held back a grade and almost half had failed a course.
- Almost half missed at least 10 days of school, one-third cut class at least 10 times and one-quarter were late at least 10 times.
- One-third were put on in-school suspension, suspended, or put on probation. More than 15 percent were expelled or told that they couldn't return.
- 11 percent were arrested.
- 8 percent spent time in a juvenile home or shelter.[1]

Without programmatic changes, the disenfranchised will continue to exist in a spiral of self-defeating behaviors that have few positive fiscal, emotional, or physical outcomes. Already ten years ago, dropouts earned slightly under $13,000 a year on average, about one-third less than high school graduates.

With respect to lifetime wages, the gap between dropouts and more educated adults is widening steadily as opportunities expand for higher skilled workers and disappear for the less skilled.[2] High school dropouts are more likely to receive public assistance than high school graduates who do not go on to college. Dropouts comprise nearly half of the heads of households on welfare. Further, the individual stresses and frustrations associated with dropping out have social implications as well: dropouts make up a disproportionate percentage of the nation's prisons and death row inmates. One research study pointed out that 82 percent of America's prisoners are high school dropouts.[3]

BELLY BEFORE SOUL

The types of changes needed to meet the needs of students who struggle in school fall into four main categories—practical, academic, social, and multisystemic. Novelist George Orwell is quoted as saying that the belly comes before the soul. Author Mark Twain reinforces this idea with "Principles have no real force except when one is well-fed." Singer Billie Holiday perhaps brings it home best with "You've got to have something to eat and a little love in your life before you can hold still for any damn body's sermon on how to behave." No matter the words used to express it, the point remains that until basic living needs are met neither children nor adults can be educated. Addressing the hierarchy of survival needs requires a multisystemic approach. Families, social service agencies, politicians, and policymakers have an equal stake with public education in the creation of functional future contributors to society. The words of author Jonathan Kozol, who has written several books about the inequalities across the American education system, create the appropriate bridge between systems and practicality. Reflecting on his extensive work with poor families from the Bronx in New York, Kozol says, "I do get scared about the physical danger from drug dealers. But it's not in the same league as the danger I feel eating an $80 lunch with my privileged friends to discuss hunger and poverty. That's when my soul feels imperiled."[4]

In my first years of teaching, I was convinced that public education should engage its efforts solely in meeting the academic needs of children. I argued that there would be no stopping point to remediating the social ills that surrounded even our suburban communities. I maintained that it was someone else's problem. I affirmed that I was a teacher, responsible for the development of the mind and not the nurturance of the body. When breakfast programs came into being, I panicked. I questioned aloud and often, "Where will it end?" Just as I wanted my first classroom of learners segregated from one another, I wanted the needs of my students to fit neatly into compartments. I wanted to ignore the rumbling stomachs, the torn clothing, and the dirty, matted hair. I wanted somebody else to deal with the body odor, the lack of money for milk or a field trip, and the lack of any learning materials in the student's home. I wanted to blame parents for failing to come to conferences, forgetting to pack lunches, and for not providing boots and mittens during harsh Wisconsin winters.

Compassion and necessity did not allow me to remain narrow-minded. I kept crackers in the cupboard to serve as emergency breakfasts. I brought bags of donated clothing and sent home anonymous packages. I wrote to social services, badgered them by phone, and gave my students hygiene lessons complete with shampoos, blow dryers, deodorant, and soap. I learned that often parents who care work hard and spend long hours away from home *because* they care. I discovered that they often have little to give beyond the shelter and clothing that their efforts provide. I found that we are wearing out the American spirit with the inequities that we allow.

I have worked with hundreds of educators from across the country. The stories that they share demonstrate an almost incomprehensible range of students, social situations, and community expectations. Educators from affluent communities are often appalled by the working conditions of their peers. Teachers from small suburban or rural cities can't conceive of the challenges inherent in providing for the vast needs of twenty or more cultures converged under one roof. The behaviors that constitute an emotional disability in a close-knit town of five thousand may not even be considered deviant in a neighboring metropolitan area. Yet the practical needs of food, shelter, money, and feelings of connectedness transcend every environment.

It's been seventeen years since my first year of teaching. I still feel that schools ought to be primarily institutions of academic instruction. I'm still afraid that by taking on too much, schools have diminished their purpose in the eyes of their communities. It is too often taken for granted that schools will meet the just-in-time (JIT) needs of students—precisely because schools do meet those needs on a daily basis. The responsibility of growing children is wholly involving. There is not often time to step out of the picture and view the process. Educators simply do what must be done to promote healthy learning. In doing so, however, dollars have been stretched thin. Schools find themselves unable to support one more unplanned-for JIT need. Hands stretch outward to corporate donations and alliances and the perception of public education as an institute in need of salvation is created. Standards grow out of the century-old debate over tracking, the fifty-year-old discovery of the impact of teacher expectations, the forty-year struggle for educational equity, and the timeless desire for highly skilled (but compliant) workers to drive the nation's economic engine. These trends have converged to create support—temporarily and for various reasons—from politicians, educators, and business leaders.[5]

The No One is Left Behind the Child plan purports to be a panacea for students who need protection from the dangers of failing public schools. In keeping with this plan, many states focus on punishing poorly performing schools, creating political opportunity but little improvement. In many states, standards and tests drive most of the curriculum; almost all states measure students against one another at a specific time rather than providing time to meet goals. High-stakes tests are being used as the sole determiners for important decisions, even for young children. Some of these tests bear little relation to the adopted standards; others are poorly constructed, not validated, too hard, politically driven, and shrouded in secrecy. These implementation policies, already breeding skepticism and resistance, seem likely to widen the gap between the educational haves and have-nots, a sad irony for a movement intended to increase equity for all children.[6]

Given the fundamental, sociological disparities that exist between learners, common sense would dictate that our government refine our social service agencies, enabling them to address the onslaught of JIT needs students experience in public schools. Practicality dictates that a communal, multi-systemic approach would not only increase academics and socialization, but would also serve to create more equitable conditions for learning. With the basic needs of their students and their students' families met, educators would have both the time and the resources to instruct a whole bevy of educational standards. Yet instead of feeding six-year-old Rosetta, whose last meal was the free lunch that she received at school yesterday, we scale back her lunch period. Instead of giving mittens to eight-year-old Skyler, we take away his recess. Instead of letting five-year-old Saul practice the social skills that we have been modeling for him, we tell him that there is no longer time for playtime in kindergarten. We simply cannot meet the needs of students who struggle in school by applying abstract and unpractical means to an end.

There can be no real answers when the tests have the power and the purse strings. A call to rebel so that our kids can excel is the first tenet of any "promising program" geared toward at-risk learners. Without a clear commitment to children as people and not products, our efforts are only Band-Aids on lacerations. David Elkind (1994), author of *The Hurried Child*, states, "When young people's developmental needs for protection and nurturance are ignored, when their human differences in growth rates and behavior are deemed deviant, and when they are given little or no space to live and grow, they are stressed."[7] A call to action necessitates a shifting of stress from defenseless children to the adults that are in the best positions to promote change—policymakers and political leaders. Author Mary Anne Raywid (2001) makes a valid point—in most places the pressure for accountability didn't come from the superintendent's office but from governors, mayors, legislatures, and the business community.[8] There is little to be gained by addressing your comments to school officials. Addressing the Rotary Club, writing letters to the editor of the local newspaper, and lobbying the legislature might be more to the point and more

effective. It's time to reinstitute the 3 Rs that really matter—
resilience, relationships, and of course, recess.

RHETORIC, REASON, AND RESULTS

For the last half of this chapter, I'd like to move beyond the
rhetoric and the reasons behind the need for reform. Not
because reform isn't integral to ultimate success but because
there are students in the hallways and the lunchrooms and
behind the desks who need real needs met right away. Teachers need ideas for reaching fifth grader Jason who day-
dreams all day. Schools need strategies for increasing family
involvement. Those that are sharing the trenches with the
disenfranchised need program ideas that work.

If one is to use what works, it is important to know what
works. Several tactics for engaging students who struggle
have already been shared, but it is also important to recognize that there are common threads among all strategies
that are consistently successful with difficult-to-reach students. Promising practices include

- Smaller schools and small class sizes
- Heterogeneous skill grouping
- Cooperative learning
- Multiple intelligences instruction
- Vocational preparation
- Early substance abuse counseling
- Ongoing pregnancy prevention and programs for expect-
  ant parents
- Flexible daily schedules
- Positive teaching and administrative staffs
- Widely shared vision of education
- Schoolwide commitment to continuous learning
- Shared decision making among all school publics

In addition, redefining authentic learning, developing new perspectives on parent involvement, and validating the efforts of alternative education programs are key components of learning systems for students who otherwise struggle in school.

Engagement depends on "authentic" learning: unless a youngster can see value in a task and perceive it as intrinsically worth doing, he's not likely to become genuinely engaged with it. This means that traditional school fare, traditionally arranged in traditionally presented academic packages (disciplines), will be unlikely to strike anyone whose heart is not set on college—or who doesn't fear parental castigation for school failure—as authentic.[9]

Constructivist learning is learning in which students construct new ideas or concepts based upon their current and past knowledge. The learner selects and transforms information, constructs hypotheses, and makes decisions, relying on a cognitive structure to do so. Constructivism works well for students who struggle in school because it is a process of making meaning personal for each learner.[10]

Constructivism involves five overarching principles. The first principle is that teachers seek and value their students' points of view. Instead of the simultaneous presentation of a concept geared toward one learning style, instruction is open-ended and the sharing of student opinions or ideas is expected. A quick way to receive a "constructivist" perspective is to ask students to create a "bumper sticker" of a new learning from a unit of study. I never fail to be amazed at the array of facts that my students have internalized as well as the creative means they use to communicate those ideas.

Second, in a constructivist learning environment, classroom activities challenge students' suppositions. One of the most effective lessons that I've witnessed involved the concept of drawing personal meaning from ecology. The teacher of the class brought in a huge bowl filled with small pieces of candy. She told her students that they were able to take as much candy as they wanted, provided that they put an equal amount of candy back into the bowl by the next day. After a week, the candy supply was nearly gone and the replacement candy was not of the quality that the first batch of goodies had been. Students were then asked to draw personal conclusions about the effect of man on nature. To do this, students had to use higher-level thinking skills to infer information, make comparisons, and generalize ideas.

Third, teachers pose problems of emerging relevance. My students used a software program this year called Building Homes of Our Own.[11] From zoning laws to environmental and ecological issues to whether or not it was fiscally prudent to locate a skate park in the backyard, students were able to work at an individualized pace to apply reasoning skills. Each facet of the software emerged as it was relevant to the student's needs. It was especially reflective of a constructivist curriculum to see the students use the home-building tool for a second time. Comments such as "So *that's* why a credit report matters," and questions such as "How do you figure out debt ratio?" reflected the students' genuine interest and enthusiasm in learning.

Fourth, teachers build lessons around primary concepts and "big" ideas. In his sixth-grade year, my son experienced a constructivist social studies classroom. Each unit of study centered on a decade of American history. Students learned the main events from each decade and also infused knowledge of pop culture, fashion, politics, songs, books, and movies from that time period into their learning. Because they were able to see a range of years from a historical perspective and then to see the subsequent decades, history took on a sense of flow that it did not have previously.

Finally, teachers who use the constructivist approach assess student learning in the context of daily teaching. When I was a teacher of students with "learning disabilities," I was fortunate enough to work with a language arts teacher who believed wholly in the concept of ongoing assessment. All assignments were centered on big ideas, had clearly defined rubrics, and included a component for student assessment. At first, it was awkward for students to participate in ongoing assessment. There were those that were always striving for "one more point" and those who set out to meet the bare minimum. Eventually, though, students began to appreciate that their efforts were assessed as a function of continuous learning rather than an ultimate paper-and-pencil test or project. Embedded assessment placed greater emphasis on the process of learning than it did the product.

In addition to benefiting from a constructivist approach to learning, students who struggle in school also profit from a responsive classroom environment. The responsive classroom approach acknowledges children's need to feel both pleasure and significance as members of a classroom community in which they feel safe, valued, and respected. The approach has six components: morning meeting, rules and logical consequences, guided discovery, classroom organization, academic choice, and assessment and reporting to parents.[12] Guided discovery, choice, and assessment within the responsive classroom are similar to the tenets of constructivism. The morning meeting, rules and logical consequences, and classroom organization are more unique to the responsive classroom approach. During the morning meeting, students gather to hear announcements, share news, welcome visitors, and play a group game. In doing so, the students learn a host of social skills. Tribes[13] offers a similar format for creating a positive classroom atmosphere.

Classroom rules are developed around positive concepts such as "Take care of friends and materials." Logical consequences are nonpunitive responses to student wrongdoing. There are three categories of consequences: you break it, you fix it; loss of a privilege; and thinking time. All three are designed to be situationally and child-specific. The Discipline with Dignity[14] and the Discipline with Love and Logic[15] curriculums work well in responsive classrooms.

In the responsive classroom, students are able to be independent as well as interactive. The classroom environment reflects a common culture that teachers and students have built over time. Furniture is typically arranged to create well-defined areas that permit children to work in a variety of configurations: alone, with partners, in small groups, as a whole group. The classroom reflects students' heritages, interests, and educational programs.

THINKING CAPS

Constructivism, responsiveness, and common sense approaches to classroom management provide authentic learning opportunities within classrooms. Research indicates that the following prove true for many at-risk youth. Too often, at-risk youth are:

- Seated farther away from the teacher
- Given less direct instruction
- Offered fewer opportunities to learn new material
- Questioned primarily at the knowledge/comprehension levels
- Not prompted when they do not know an answer
- Given less praise
- Rewarded for inappropriate behavior
- Criticized more frequently
- Given less feedback
- Interrupted more often
- Given less eye contact and other nonverbal communication of attentiveness and responsiveness[16]

Common sense, then, would dictate that if these practices were eliminated, success rates would increase. Common sense also urges educators to put on Thinking CAPs and address Creativity, Appreciation, and Peer relationships as part of the everyday classroom environment. Academic creativity is a way of thinking about, learning, and producing information in school subjects such as science, mathematics, and history. Creative thinking and learning involve such abilities as evaluation (especially the ability to sense problems, inconsistencies, and missing elements); divergent production (e.g., fluency, flexibility, originality, and elaboration); and redefinition. Creative learning is a natural, healthy human process that occurs when people become curious and excited. In contrast, learning by authority requires students to use thinking skills such as recognition, memory, and logical reasoning—the abilities most frequently assessed by traditional tests of intelligence and scholastic aptitude. To enhance creativity, educators should make assignments that call for original work, independent learning, self-initiated projects, and experimentation. Using curriculum materials that provide progressive warm-up experiences, procedures that permit one thing to lead to another, and activities that make creative thinking both legitimate and rewarding make it easier for teachers to provide opportunities for creative learning.[17] In addition, it is important for teachers to make certain that students have the appropriate supplies to enact their creativity. Paper, fun markers, special scissors, stamps, and other atypical classroom art supplies will allow all students equal access to the equipment needed to bring their learning to life.

Expressing appreciation is among the most powerful tools that every educator has at her disposal. Child development researchers Betty Hart and Todd Risley (1995) found that children who are the most intelligent, self-confident, and flexible at ages six to eight had experienced five times more positive than negative interchanges with their parents by age three. By the age of three, the children who would thrive had received an average of around 500,000 positive interactions.[18] Appreciation is most effective when it is directly linked to a teacher's genuine personal feelings as they relate to a certain set of classroom behaviors. For example, instead of telling Zeb that he is a good worker, a teacher might comment, "Zeb, I appreciated the way that you got your paper and pencil out, opened your book right up, and completed ten problems." When used appropriately, appreciation affirms a student's own joy in performing and reinforces their resiliency in more difficult times. Because life continually requires us to attend to problems and break-downs, it gets very easy to see in life only what is broken and in need of fixing. Sometimes, when students struggle for too long, they, too, are seen as needy—the whole is lost for the part of the student that needs "fixing." Appreciating the whole is what ultimately builds strong children. It is appreci-ation that makes life satisfying and that makes relationships strong enough to accommodate differences and disagree-ments. Thinkers and researchers in many different fields have reached similar conclusions: healthy relationships need a core of mutual appreciation.[19]

The final facet of a Thinking CAP is positive Peer relation-ships. All of the suggestions already made regarding relation-ship building, climate control, and positive communication will assist a teacher with developing a web of interconnected learners. Another program, Positive Peer Groups (PPG), has operated for the last nine years in grades 5–9 in both public and parochial school settings throughout northeastern Ohio. The PPG model was designed and is currently being imple-mented by the Prevention Initiatives Division of Prevention Systems Intervention (PSI) Affiliates, Inc., a private consor-tium of psychologists, educators, and prevention specialists who work in partnership with the Cleveland Catholic diocese and other public schools. PSI was founded to deliver a research-based, multitiered program of teacher, parent, and staff training; consultation; and, most important, direct ser-vices to students. The PPG program has recently begun serv-ing students in several public school systems, especially those schools in the poorest urban areas within the district. Over the nine years in which the program has been implemented, it has come to include over 100 schools and to serve more than one thousand students annually.

PPG is a leadership training program that helps alien-ated and disengaged students bond to school by giving them the opportunity to participate in school-oriented service activities and, in the process, to form constructive affiliations with peers who are involved in the same efforts. The intense power of the peer group is used to help students develop socially positive attitudes and a mature outlook toward school. There is strong evidence that this approach has an impact on such problems as school failure, school violence, delinquency, and substance abuse.

In the program, students are taught to develop independence by participating in group activities focusing on work, discipline, and responsibility. Adult facilitators encourage participation and involvement as the students learn to solve problems, make their own decisions, plan, and set measurable goals. The facilitators help the students to understand that these activities have allowed them to become contributing and responsible members of the school society.

Work, discipline, and responsibility interact synergistically as individual students become a team. The students are in control: facilitators act as a support system, providing training and assistance only when needed. It is the students' responsibility to identify a problem within the school community and then propose and execute a solution to that problem as a group. Identification occurs first with the group and then with the school. Students are introduced to the social structure of the school as adults would be and are asked to shoulder adult responsibilities within a team of their peers.

Integral to the success of this program is the inclusion of positive peer leaders in each group. These students themselves benefit from the program as their social skills, commitment to service, and dedication to helping their peers are all greatly enhanced as a result of their involvement. Although their role as peer models is not made explicit, their participation is central to the program's success.

While the PPG program addresses students' individual problems, it also serves to target schoolwide issues of concern. The identification of these systemwide concerns determines the types of service activities the student groups embark upon. For example, one group of students participating in the program designed a Racial Diversity Awareness Day to bring the issue of racial tension to the attention of students, teachers, and parents. Another group was particularly concerned about teen alcohol abuse. Their solution was to design a comprehensive Drinking Awareness Week. A different group, reacting to the media's intensive coverage of high school violence in general and to local physical fighting in particular, designed a weeklong Anti-Violence Campaign. Students participated in workshops and activities to help them respond more effectively to those who bully and threaten. Guest speakers addressed issues of safety and weapons.

Culminating activities for many Positive Peer Groups focus on peer tutoring and mentoring programs. These programs are excellent opportunities for disengaged students to occupy high-profile roles. Rather than always being the object of such special services as tutoring and counseling, in these programs the troubled students themselves become the tutors and mentors. They develop a constructive reputation while building their academic, organizational, and decision-making skills.[20]

When I was a middle school principal, we had two programs designed to link students to positive role models. In one program, high school students lent their academic talents to assisting middle school students in need of tutoring. While primarily academic in focus, the program naturally included social components that were equally, if not more, vital to the middle school students' success. A second program involved our eighth grade students being "pen pals" for first graders with emerging writing skills. It was so touching to see the rough and tough eighth graders gently leading wide-eyed first graders through the building at the end-of-year culminating activity. Students have proven, time and again, that they will live up—or down—to our levels of expectation. In a world where inter-reliance is key to survival, it behooves us all to keep our expectations high.

HEADS, I WIN . . . TAILS, YOU LOSE

On school picture day, Jayden forgot her envelope and money and her mother brought them to school. Later that same day, her mom made the trip again to bring in a project that Jayden needed in order to receive credit in science class. Still later, Jayden's mom returned to school at the end of the day to drive Jayden and a friend to the mall. Yet many would call Jayden's mother "uninvolved" and they would imply that she is not interested in her daughter's education. You see, in all the years I've known Jayden, I've only met her mother once, during the very first semester that my relationship with her daughter began. It was as if she sized me up at that conference, decided that I was trustworthy, and determined that no future conferences were necessary.

Then there is Latrell's father. He bustled in to every single parent-teacher conference that the school has hosted. He nodded, took notes, and affirmed that he would help Latrell at home as necessary. But history showed that he had difficulty following through on his promises to help organize his son and monitor his study habits.

Nathan's mother never came to a single parent-teacher conference. She never phoned. Yet she signed the assignment notebook faithfully each evening for her son. Nathan remarked that she helped him structure his homework time and insisted upon hearing about his progress

So, which parent was more involved? One popular notion is that parents are "involved" when they actively participate in school-sponsored activities or help their children in ways that are visible to others. A vision of involvement solely dependent upon visibility combined with action is an impediment to effectively engaging the parents of students who struggle in school. Parents who have had unsuccessful school careers may feel a great deal of anxiety and intimidation when meeting with teachers. In addition, parents tend to view their children as extensions of themselves and will avoid situations where they can expect criticisms of themselves or their children. The social environment of a school may also make parents uncomfortable. The presence of parents with higher socioeconomic status may make parents of lower socioeconomic classes feel self-conscious. Tangentially, issues of transportation and child care can impede direct school involvement.[21]

Research on family involvement has indicated that interventions that involve parents as partners are more effective in building academic and social skills within children. It is important to recognize that parents from all backgrounds want their children to be successful in school. However, many parents report that they need more guidance about how to help their child.[22]

Communication is vital to forming home-school collaborations. The key to improving communication lies not only in meeting parents where they are but also in accepting them as they are. Establish rapport and highlight the fact that the best interests of the students should always be in the forefront both at home and in school. Provide a broad range of information and activities that will make parents feel involved even when low levels of commitment are required. Contributing a package of cookies for an event, for example, is very different from having to attend that event and sell the cookies.

When working with students who struggle in school, it is also important to accept the hard fact that some parents are not concerned with education. I once went on a home visit for a new middle school student who was experiencing many behavioral problems. Her mother, who had refused to come to school for the conference, proudly told me that her daughter's very first word was an expletive. In fact, her mother wrote this information on the child's enrollment form with great relish. In the presence of her smirking daughter, the mother calmly informed the school psychologist and me that she did not feel that school was a priority, was herself a dropout, and saw no reason for her daughter to exhibit any social skills beyond the rudimentary ones that she had already developed.

Sometimes, too, students personalize their parents' lack of involvement. I once had a student who was behind in her work request, "Please call my grandma and tell her about it. Don't call my mom . . . she won't make me do it. But my grandma will." Other students tell me that their parents will come to a conference—and then the students slink into their seats with heads down after the parents fail to show up. Others tell me that their parents laugh when the principal calls home, that their parents were never good at math, either, or that their parents say that they do not have to do homework. It is important to tell such students clearly that there are other models of parenting, that they are not pre-destined to embrace all things that their parents value, and even that they are responsible for growing beyond their current situation. My toughest student ever, Brian, cried when I told him that his father's abuse was not his fault, that he was capable of being a good father someday and that it was not inevitable that his life would meet the gloom-and-doom predictions of the father who called him names and denigrated him daily. Brian cried that day because it hurt to hear the truth aloud. More important, though, he cried because he received a realistic message of hope. His tears released him from the future that he mistakenly thought had to be his. Meet parents where they are, accept them as they are, but let them go if need be. There is an old admonishment to never deprive someone of hope, for it may be all that they have. Teachers are capable of extending a student's vision to environments more evolved than those they reside in while in school. At least, let's hope so.

WHAT'S MY ALTERNATIVE?

During my tenure as a middle school principal, I witnessed the most promising middle-level practices infuse themselves into high schools—block scheduling, student advisory time, and portfolio assessment are just a few of the "new" strategies being employed for the purpose of creating more successful graduates. Of course, high schools do not acknowledge the roots of their reform. Middle schools invariably operate under the "Cinderella" complex and fail to be acknowledged for their vast contributions. It is, I believe, the same for the plethora of alternative educational environments that have sprung up across our nation. Alternative schools generally offer smaller class sizes and adult mentors for each student, engage in individualized instruction geared toward maximal learning, and provide a strong link between students and the community services that are available to them. Why, then, with all of this positive practice, are alternative schools viewed like the smallest puppy at the pound?

Many alternative schools start as solutions to the problems of disruption and alienation in "big schools" and it is the big schools that decide who should go to the alternative school. What's more, the students they send there are not their good students or even their average ones. Instead, they are the young people that conventional high schools have given up on. The premise behind the transfer is that the sending school is not the problem; the student is the problem. A distinctive, almost punitive tone is set for the alternative school. Too often, the litmus paper of success is a smooth transition back to a traditional learning environment. This reinforces the idea that the traditional environment is more desirable then the alternative one. Further, it denies a quality educational setting to a heterogeneous group of students.[23]

Alternative schools do not need to perpetuate the notion that they exist for students with little desire to learn. Instead, alternative environments should be established for all of the nontraditional learners within a school system. The choice of an alternative school should be as appealing as a charter school geared toward specific student needs. The business of alternative schools is to create powerful, engaging programs that stretch students in ways never envisioned. Alternative schools can create programs so different from those of standard schools and learning communities, so engaging to students that they require new forms of space.[24] Indeed, I often am approached by students, especially those who learn outside of the typical intelligence areas, begging to be in my class. Because the enrollment in my class is capped by the district, I am only able to educate them to learn about their personal styles, provide them with information as needed, and encourage my students to continue to serve as role models for the concept that "different is not less and can even be more."

SEE HOW THEY RUN

Alternative schools do not need to be underfunded programs housed in locations adjacent to "real" learning environments. Students who struggle in school do not need to be the passive majority. Those who hear a different drummer ought to be marching. The moment is upon us to stop the high-stakes testing insanity and to send the standardistos packing. It is time to restore passion and principles in our schools, creativity in our children, and joy in our relationships. The real hope for all students who struggle in school lies in the hands of the people who care for them. It's time for them to do as Mark Twain says and "Dance like nobody's watching." And perhaps, if enough glass slippers are left to sparkle after the dance, the discovery of what's best for children will be made. Then, and only then, will there truly be no child left behind.

APPENDIX A

Armstrong, Thomas. 2000. *Multiple Intelligences in the Classroom.* Alexandria, VA: Association of Supervision and Curriculum Development.

Chapman, Carolyn. 1993. *If the Shoe Fits* . . . Glenview, IL: IRI Skylight Publishing.

Delisle, Deb and Jim Delisle. 1997. *Growing Good Kids: 28 Activities to Enhance Self-Awareness, Compassion and Leadership.* Minneapolis: Free Spirit Publishing.

Foster-Harrison, Elizabeth. 2000. *Energizers and Icebreakers: For All Ages and Stages.* Minneapolis: Educational Media Corporation.

Jackson, T. 1993. *Activities That Teach.* Salt Lake City: Red Rock Publishing.

Kaufeldt, Martha. 1999. *Begin with the Brain.* Tucson: Zephyr Press.

Lazear, David. 1998. *Eight Ways of Knowing: Teaching for Multiple Intelligences.* Glenview, IL: Skylight Publishing.

Lazear, David. 2001. *Pathways of Learning: Teaching Students and Parents about Multiple Intelligences.* Tucson: Zephyr Press.

Lazear, David. 2003. *Eight Ways of Teaching: The Artistry of Teaching with Multiple Intelligences.* Glenview, IL: Skylight Publishing.

McElherne, Linda Nason. 1998. *Jumpstarters: Quick Classroom Activities that Develop Self-Esteem and Cooperation.* Minneapolis: Free Spirit Publishing.

Miller, Jamie. 1998. *10 Minute Life Lessons for Kids.* New York: HarperCollins.

Newstrom, John and Edward Scannell. 1997. *The Big Book of Team Building Games.* New York: McGraw-Hill.

Senn, J. A. 1994. *325 Creative Prompts for Personal Journals.* New York: Scholastic.

APPENDIX B
Life in the Wright Family

One day the Wright family decided to take a vacation. The first thing they had to decide was who would be left at home since there was not enough room in the Wright family car for all of them. Mr. Wright decided that Aunt Linda Wright would be the one left at home. Of course this made Aunt Linda Wright so mad that she left the house immediately, yelling, "It will be a right cold day before I return!"

The Wright family now bundled up the children, Tommy Wright, Susan Wright, Timmy Wright, and Shelly Wright, and got in the car and left. Unfortunately, as they turned out of the driveway, someone had left a trash can in the street so they had to turn right around and stop the car. They told Tommy Wright to get out of the car and move the trash can so they could get going. Tommy took so long that they almost left him in the street. Once the Wright family got on the road, Mother Wright wondered if she had left the stove on. Father Wright told her not to worry, he had checked the stove and she had not left it on. As they turned right at the corner, everyone started to think about other things that they might have left undone.

No need to worry now, they were off on a right fine vacation. When they arrived at the gas station, Father Wright put gas in the car and they discovered that he had left his wallet at home. So Timmy Wright ran home to get the money that was left behind. After Timmy had left, Susan Wright started to feel sick. She left the car, saying that she had to throw up.

This of course got Mother Wright's attention and she left the car in a hurry. Shelly Wright wanted to watch Susan get sick, so she left the car too. Father Wright was left with Tommy Wright, who was playing a game in the backseat.

With all of this going on, Father Wright decided that this was not the right time to take a vacation, so he gathered up all of the family and left the gas station as quickly as he could. When he arrived home, he turned left into the driveway and said, "I wish the Wright family had never left the house today!"

NOTES

Chapter One

1. Druian, G. and J. Butler. 1987. "Effective Schooling Practices and At-Risk Youth: What Research Shows." *School Improvement Series, Northwest Regional Educational Laboratory,* November 1987. Online. Cited 9 September 2002. Available from <http://nwrel.org/scpd/sirs/1/topsyn1.html>.

2. National Center for Educational Statistics. 1997. "Confronting the Odds: Students At-Risk and the Pipeline to Higher Education." Online. National Center for Educational Statistics. Cited 1 September 2002. Available from <http://nces.ed.gov/pubs98/98094.html>.

3. Henderson, N. (ed.) and B. Bernard and N. Sharp-Light. 1999. *Resiliency in Action: Practical Ideas for Overcoming Risks and Building Strengths in Youth, Families, and Communities:* Resiliency in Action. Info available at www.resiliency.com.

4. "Developmental Assets: An Overview." Online. Search Institute. Cited 1 September 2002. Available from <http://www.search-institute.org>.

5. Loken, J. "Teacher, I Can't Learn in School." Online. Cited 11-01-02. Available from <http://www.northernlightsdesign.com/teacher/#anchor1291855>.

6. Kendrick, C. 2000–2003. "The Hurried Child, Revisited." Online. Family Education Network. Cited 1 September 2002. Available from <http://www.familyeducation.net>.

7. Levin, H. 1986. *Educational Reform for Disadvantaged Students: An Emerging Crisis.* Washington, D.C.: NEA Search.

8. England, C. 2003. *None of Our Business: Why Business Models Don't Work in Schools.* Portsmouth, NH: Heinemann.

9. Henderson, J. "Essential Conditions." Online. California School Redesign Network. Cited 1 September 2002. Available from <http://www.stanford.edu/dept/SUSE/csrn/resources/essential/>.

10. Covey, S. 1990. *Seven Habits of Highly Effective People.* New York: Simon & Schuster.

11. Palmer, J. (ed.) *Young Children in Poverty: A Statistical Update.* 1999. New York: Columbia University.

12. U.S. Conference of Mayors. 1997. *A Status Report on Hunger and Homelessness in America's Cities.* Info available at www.usmayors.org/uscm/homeless/hunger99.pdf.

13. *Child Maltreatment 2000.* (2002) U.S. Department of Health and Human Services, Administration on Children, Youth and Families. Washington, DC: U.S. Government Printing Office.

14. Lent, R. and G. Pipkin. (eds). 2003. *Silent No More: Voices of Courage in American Schools.* Portsmouth, NH: Heinemann.

Chapter Two

1. *American Heritage Dictionary,* 4th ed., s.v. "climate."

2. Marzano, Robert and D. Pickering. 1992. *Dimensions of Learning.* Alexandria, VA: Association for Supervision and Curriculum Development.

3. Jackson, T. 1993. *Activities That Teach.* Salt Lake City: Red Rock Publishing.

4. Gunter, M., T. Estes, and J. Schwab. 1999. *Instruction: A Models Approach.* Boston: Allyn & Bacon.

5. Thibodeau, Amy. 1998. "Educator's Cheapbook: PB&J Programming." Online. Museum of Science (Boston). Cited 1 November 2002. Available from <http://www.mos.org/learn_more/ed_res/cheapbook/pbj>.

6. Palmer, Parker. 1998. *The Courage to Teach*. San Francisco, CA: Jossey-Bass.

7. Palmer, Parker. See note 6.

8. Loui, Michael. 1999. "Courage in the Classroom." Speech delivered to Graduate Teacher Certificate Ceremony, 26 April. University of Illinois at Urbana-Champaign, IL.

9. Palmer, Parker. See note 6.

10. *Performance Learning Systems: Successful Teaching for Acceptance of Responsibility*. 2002. Performance Learning Systems. <http://www.plsweb.com/sec03_graduate/courses/success.htm>. Database online, created 2 April. Available from Performance Learning Plus, Number 19.

11. Hanratty and Associates. 2002. "Time Is Becoming Critical to the Success of Workers." Online. Hanratty and Associates. Cited Summer 2002. Available from <http://hanrattyassoc.com/pages/Summer2002_NL/SM_Critical2Success.html>.

Chapter Three

1. Kofman, Fred and Peter Senge. 1995. *Learning Organizations: Developing Cultures for Tomorrow's Workplace*. Edited by Sarita Chawla and John Renesch. Portland, OR: Productivity Press.

2. Kofman, Fred and Peter Senge. See Note 1.

3. Kofman, Fred and Peter Senge. See Note 1.

4. Gibbs, Jeanne. 1978. *Tribes: A Process for Peer Involvement*. Oakland, CA: Center Source Publications.

5. Kofman, Fred and Peter Senge. See Note 1.

6. Bhanumurthy, Kalyanalakshmy. 1999. "The Sharp Edge of Competition." *The Hindu*, 7 February.

7. Josephson, Michael, Tom Dowd, and Val Peter. 2001. *Parenting to Build Character in Your Teen*. Boys Town, NE: Boys Town Press.

8. Lickona, Thomas. 1992. *Educating for Character*. New York: Bantam Books.

9. Johnson, Roger and David Johnson. 1994. *Creativity and Collaborative Learning*. Edited by Jacqueline Thousand, Richard Villa, and Ann Nevin. Baltimore: Paul H. Brookes Press.

10. Johnson, Roger and David Johnson. See Note 9.

11. Johnson, Roger and David Johnson. See Note 9.

12. Johnson, Roger and David Johnson. See Note 9.

13. Beveridge, 'Alim. 2002. "Leap In: Practicing Empathy and Perspective Taking Through Simulation." Master's thesis, Stanford University, Stanford, CA. Available online at <http://ldt.stanford.edu/~alim/leapin/>.

14. Further information available at <http://www.charactercounts.org>.

15. IALAC story available at <http://www.os-iti.org/os/Snowflake.pdf>.

16. Lenehan, Arthur (compiler). 1994. *The Best of Bits and Pieces*. Fairfield, NJ: The Economics Press.

17. Brady, Marion. 2000. "The Standards Juggernaut." *Phi Delta Kappan* 81, no. 9 (May): 648–651.

18. Badnarik, Michael. 2000. *The Project Zero Classroom: New Approaches to Understanding*. Cambridge, MA: Harvard Graduate School of Education, Project Zero.

19. Curwin, Richard and Allen Mendler. 1999. "Zero Tolerance for Zero Tolerance." *Phi Delta Kappan* 81, no. 2 (October): 119–120. Online. Accessed 1 December 2002. Available from <http://www.pdkintl.org/kappan/kcur9910.htm>.

20. Curwin, Richard and Allan Mendler. See Note 19.

21. Gardner, Howard. 1995. "Reflections on Multiple Intelligences: Myths and Messages." *Phi Delta Kappan* 78, no 3 (November).

22. Gardner, Howard. See Note 21.

23. Ludy, T. 1988. "A History of Teaching Machines." *American Psychologist* 43, no. 9.

24. Worthington, Valerie. "Individualizing Education—Theoretical Rationale." Online. LetsNet. Cited 1 December 2002. Available from <http://www.commtechlab.msu.edu/sites/letsnet/noframes/bigideas/b8/b8theor.html>.

Chapter Four

1. Information available at <http://www.pbs.org/merrow/tv/add>.

2. Silverman, Linda Kreger. 2000. *Counseling the Gifted and Talented.* Denver: Love Publishing.

3. Information available at <http://www.atriskeducation.net>.

4. Silverman, Linda Kreger. 2002. *Upside Down Brilliance: The Visual Spatial Learner.* Denver: Deleon Publishing.

5. Strip, Carol and Gretchen Hirsch. 2000. *Helping Gifted Children Soar: A Practical Guide for Parents and Teachers.* Scottsdale, AZ: Great Potential Press.

6. Molvig, Dianne. 1996. "The Good Doctor Says: 'Lighten Up!'" *Wisconsin Lawyer,* May.

7. Patterson, James. "Just a Dash of Humor for Speaking and Business Success." Online. The Cogent Communicator. Cited 1 February 2003. Available from <http://www2.pvc.maricopa.edu/~patterson/Humor%20in%20Business%20Article.doc>.

8. Marzano, Robert and D. Pickering. 1992. *Dimensions of Learning.* Alexandria, VA: Association for Supervision and Curriculum Development.

9. Syverson, Peg. "The Five Dimensions." Online. Computer Writing and Research Lab, University of Texas at Austin. Cited 1 January 2003. Available from <http:// www.cwrl.utexas.edu/~syverson/olr/dimensions.html>.

Chapter Five

1. Schwartz, Wendy. "New Information on Youth Who Drop Out: Why They Leave and What Happens to Them." Online. Kidsource. Cited 24 September 2002. Available from <www.kidsource.com/kidsource/content4/youth.drop. out.html>.

2. Schwartz, Wendy. 1995. "School Dropouts: New Information about an Old Problem." Online. ERIC Clearinghouse of Urban Education. Cited 21 April 2002. Available from <http://eric-web.tc.columbia.edu/digest/dig109.asp>.

3. Dropout information compiled from: U.S. Department of Education, National Center for Educational Statistics. 1998. *Dropout Rates in the U.S.,* Washington, D.C. <http:// www.dropoutprevention.org>, ERIC Digest No. 109 *School Dropouts,* ERIC Digest No. 125 *Student Truancy,* and <http:// www.georgiafamilyconnection.org/policybp/ causeshsdropout.doc>.

4. Obtained online (9-5-03) at www.josephsoninstitute.org/ quotes/quotefairness.htm.

5. Gratz, Donald B. 2000. "High Standards for Whom?" *Phi Delta Kappan* 81, no. 9 (May): 681–687. Online. Cited 11 April 2003. Available from <http://www.pdkintl.org/ kappan/kgra0005.htm>.

6. Gratz, Donald. See Note 5.

7. Elkind, David. 1994. *Ties That Stress: The New Family Imbalance.* Cambridge, MA: Harvard University Press.

8. Raywid, Mary Anne. 2001. "What to Do with Students Who Are Not Succeeding." *Phi Delta Kappan* 82, no. 8 (April).

9. Raywid, Mary Anne. See Note 8.

10. Brooks, Jaqueline Grennon and Martin Brooks. 1999. "In Search of Understanding: The Case for Constructivist Classrooms." Online. Association for Supervision and Curriculum Development. Cited 24 September 2002. Available from <http://www.ascd.org/readingroom/books/brooks99toc.html>.

11. *Building Homes of Our Own* was funded through private sector grants for use by middle school systems. For more information about the game, go to <http://www.Homes-OfOurOwn.org>. Media Options Inc., a Chicago/LA company, developed the game. For other program development details go to www.mediaop.com.

12. Horsch, Patricia, Jie Qi Chen, and Donna Nelson. 1999. "Rules and Rituals: Tools for Creating a Respectful, Caring, Learning Community." *Phi Delta Kappan* 81, no. 3 (November).

13. Gibbs, Jeanne. 1978. *Tribes: A Process for Peer Involvement.* Oakland, CA: Center Source Publications.

14. Curwin, Richard and Allen Mendler. 1999. *Discipline with Dignity.* Alexandria, VA: Association for Supervision and Curriculum Development.

15. Fay, Jim and Foster Cline. *Discipline with Love and Logic.* Golden, CO: Love and Logic Press.

16. Further information available at <http://www.sedl.org/rural/atrisk/practices.html>.

17. Torrance, E. and K. Goff. 1989. "A Quiet Revolution." *Journal of Creative Behavior* 2, no. 23.

18. Hart, Betty and Todd Risley. 1995. *Meaningful Differences.* Baltimore: Paul H. Brookes Publishing.

19. Material from *The Seven Challenges* workbook by Dennis Rivers included with permission of the author. Further information available at <http://www.coopcomm.org/workbook.htm>.

20. Rosenberg, Steven, Loren McKeon, and Thomas Dinero. 1999. "Positive Peer Solutions: One Answer for the Rejected Student." *Phi Delta Kappan*, 81, no. 2 (October): 114–118.

21. Karther, Diane and Frances Lowden. 1997. "Fostering Effective Parent Involvement." *Contemporary Education* 69, no. 1 (fall).

22. Christianson, S. L., M. Sinclair, D. Evelo, and M. Thurlow. 1995. *Tip the Balance: Practices and Policies That Influence School Engagement for Youth at Risk for Dropping Out.* Minneapolis: University of Minnesota, College of Education and Human Development, Institute on Community Integration (ERIC Document reproduction service no. ED398673).

23. Gregory, Tom. 2001. "Fear of Success? Ten Ways Alternative Schools Pull Their Punches." *Phi Delta Kappan*, 82, no. 8 (April): 577.

24. Gregory, Tom. See Note 23.

BIBLIOGRAPHY

Covey, Stephen. 1990. *Seven Habits of Highly Effective People.* New York: Simon & Schuster.

Curwin, Richard and Allen Mendler. 1999. *Discipline with Dignity.* Alexandria, VA: Association for Supervision and Curriculum Development.

Doyon, Juanita. 2003. *Not with Our Kids You Don't! Ten Strategies to Save Our Schools.* Portsmouth, NH: Heinemann.

England, Crystal. 2003. *None of Our Business: Why Business Models Don't Work in Schools.* Portsmouth, NH: Heinemann.

Fay, Jim and Foster Cline. *Discipline with Love and Logic.* Golden, CO: Love and Logic Press.

Gibbs, Jeanne. 1978. *Tribes: A Process for Peer Involvement.* Oakland, CA: Center Source Publications.

Johnson, Roger and David Johnson. 1994. *Creativity and Collaborative Learning.* Edited by Jacqueline Thousand, Richard Villa, and Ann Nevin. Baltimore: Paul H. Brookes Press.

Josephson, Michael, Tom Dowd, and Val Peter. 2001. *Parenting to Build Character in Your Teen.* Boys Town, NE: Boys Town Press.

Kofman, Fred and Peter Senge. 1995. *Learning Organizations: Developing Cultures for Tomorrow's Workplace.* Edited by Sarita Chawla and John Renesch. Portland, OR: Productivity Press.

Kohn, Alfie. 1997. *Beyond Discipline: From Compliance to Community.* Alexandria, VA: Association for Supervision and Curriculum Development.

Kohn, Alfie. 1992. *No Contest: The Case Against Competition*. New York: Houghton Mifflin.

Lazear, David. 2003. *Higher Order Thinking, The MI Way! Moving Students' Thinking to Higher-Order Realms*. Brookline, MA: Zephyr Press.

Lazear, David. 2003. *You're Smarter Than You Think! The Ultimate Guide to Awakening Your Multiple Intelligences*. For publication information see <http://www.davidlazear.com>.

Lent, R. and G. Pipkin (eds). 2003. *Silent No More: Voices of Courage in American Schools*. Portsmouth, NH: Heinemann.

Lickona, Thomas. 1992. *Educating for Character*. New York: Bantam Books.

Marzano, Robert and D. Pickering. 1992. *Dimensions of Learning*. Alexandria, VA: Association for Supervision and Curriculum Development.

Palmer, Parker. 1998. *The Courage to Teach*. San Francisco, CA: Jossey-Bass.

Ohanian, Susan. 1999. *One Size Fits Few: The Folly of Educational Standards*. Portsmouth, NH: Heinemann.

Ohanian, Susan. 2002. *What Happened to Recess and Why Are Our Children Struggling in Kindergarten?* New York: McGraw-Hill.

Silverman, Linda Kreger. 2002. *Upside Down Brilliance: The Visual Spatial Learner*. Denver: Deleon Publishing.

Sizer, Theodore and N. Sizer. 2000. *The Students Are Watching: Schools and the Moral Contract*. Boston: Beacon Press.

Strip, Carol and Gretchen Hirsch. 2000. *Helping Gifted Children Soar: A Practical Guide for Parents and Teachers*. Scottsdale, AZ: Great Potential Press.